TOP 10 GRAN CANARIA

LUCY CORNE

EY[illegible]

Left **Las Palmas by night** Right **Cactus garden, Jardín Botánico Viera y Clavijo**

LONDON, NEW YORK,
MELBOURNE, MUNICH AND DELHI
www.dk.com

Produced by DP Services,
31 Ceylon Road, London W14 0PY

Printed and bound in China by Leo Paper Products Ltd

First published in Great Britain in 2006 by Dorling Kindersley Limited
80 Strand, London WC2R 0RL
A Penguin Company

14 15 16 17 10 9 8 7 6 5 4 3 2 1

Reprinted with revisions 2008, 2010, 2012, 2014

A CIP catalogue record is available from the British Library.

ISBN 978 1 40932 625 0

Within each Top 10 list in this book, no hierarchy of quality or popularity is implied. All 10 are, in the editor's opinion, of roughly equal merit.

Contents

Gran Canaria's Top 10

The information in this DK Eyewitness Top 10 Travel Guide is checked regularly.

Every effort has been made to ensure that this book is as up-to-date as possible at the time of going to press. Some details, however, such as telephone numbers, opening hours, prices, gallery hanging arrangements and travel information are liable to change. The publishers cannot accept responsibility for any consequences arising from the use of this book, nor for any material on third party websites, and cannot guarantee that any website address in this book will be a suitable source of travel information. We value the views and suggestions of our readers very highly. Please write to: Publisher, DK Eyewitness Travel Guides, Dorling Kindersley, 80 Strand, London WC2R 0RL, Great Britain, or email: travelguides@dk.com.

Cover: Front – **Dorling Kindersley:** Neville Walker bl; **Getty Images:** Michele Falzone main. Spine – **Dorling Kindersley:** Pawel Wojcik b. Back – **Dorling Kindersley:** Tony Souter c, cr; Pawel Wojcik cl.

ft **Agüimes** Right **Playa del Inglés**

Around Gran Canaria

Streetsmart

: **Camel rides** Right **The dramatic road between Ayacata and Artenara**

***Note**: throughout this guide, the island's capital, Las Palmas de Gran Canaria, is referred to by the short form of its name, Las Palmas.*

GRAN CANARIA'S TOP 10

Top 10 Gran Canaria Highlights

Gran Canaria has often been described as "a continent in miniature", and with good reason. Within just 1,500 sq km (580 sq miles) you can travel from the rugged northern coast through verdant laurel forests and extinct volcanoes to the emblematic central peaks, reaching almost 2,000 m (6,562 ft) above sea level, before you descend again through ancient pine woodlands into the deep ravines of the south and west, which peter out as the arid landscape gives way to glorious golden beaches. The fine sand and perfect climate ensure that the island is no stranger to tourists, but there are as many oppportunities to escape the crowds as there are to encounter them in this magical Atlantic haven.

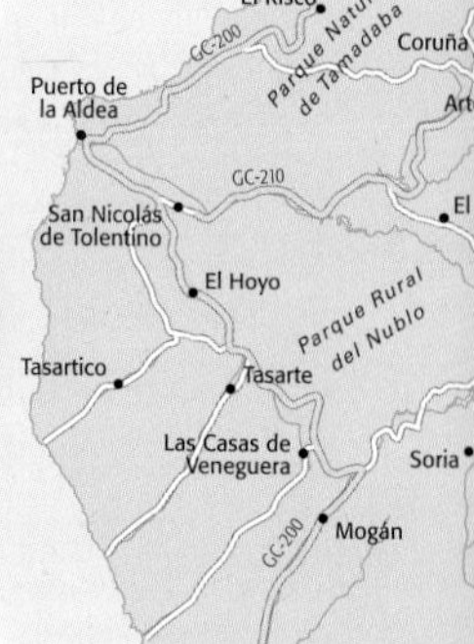

1 Casa de Colón

Trace Columbus's epic journeys in this atmospheric museum based in the 15th-century governor's house where the Atlantic explorer stayed en route to the New World *(see pp8–9)*.

2 Catedral de Santa Ana

Standing proud in Las Palmas's historic centre, the cathedral has been an emblem of the city since the Spanish conquered the island. Its intermittent construction over 400 years explains the magnificent potpourri of styles that singles it out as one of the most important artistic monuments in Gran Canaria *(see pp10–11)*.

3 Museo Canario

Since they died out soon after the Spanish Conquest, there is little information on how the Guanches (early Canarios) lived. Gain insight at the Museo Canario, a one-stop exploration of the mysteries of ancient Canarian culture *(see pp12–13)*.

4 Jardín Botánico Viera y Clavijo

Spain's largest botanical garden is a mixed bouquet of endemic and tropical plants. Giant lizards bask in the sun while songbirds chirrup in the laurel and pine plantations *(see pp14–17)*.

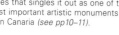

Preceding pages **A view of Gran Canaria's mountainous interior, with Roque Bentayga in the middle distance**

5 Maspalomas

Maspalomas, with its golden dunes, is both a tourist resort and an area of stunning natural beauty, visited by holidaymakers and migrating birds alike *(see pp18–19)*.

6 Teror

Set in an area of outstanding natural beauty, this quiet, architecturally exquisite Canarian town has deep historical roots. It's also home to a tasty local variety of *chorizo* sausage *(see pp20–23)*.

7 La Cumbre

Wherever you are in the island's central mountains, there are awe-inspiring views of La Cumbre's high ridges and strange rock formations *(see pp24–25)*.

8 Caldera de Bandama

A reminder of the island's volcanic origins, this deep crater is an easy visit from Las Palmas. Enjoy the fabulous views, or hike down to the crater floor *(see pp26–27)*.

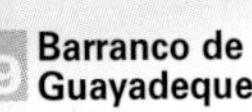

9 Barranco de Guayadeque

Guanche cave homes line the sides of this breathtaking ravine; the modern troglodytes are easier to visit *(see pp28–29)*.

10 Puerto de las Nieves

Scores of visitors pass through Puerto de las Nieves daily en route to Tenerife, but this pretty fishing village is a destination in its own right. Watch the boats, enjoy a seafood lunch, and unwind *(see pp30–31)*.

TOP 10 Casa de Colón

One of the capital's most delightful buildings is a wonderful museum where the main focus is the discovery of America. In the 15th century, the governor's home stood on this site, though the building has changed considerably since then. While not certain, it's very likely that this is where Christopher Columbus stayed in 1492 before he set off in search of a shortcut to India and unwittingly stumbled across America instead.

Courtyard, Casa de Colón

Cho Zacarias on C/Audencia is a quiet place for an upmarket lunch.

Don't forget to visit the Ermita de San Antonio Abad, 50 m (164 ft) from the museum. Columbus is said to have prayed here before crossing the Atlantic.

- *C/Colón 1*
- *Map M5*
- *928 31 23 73*
- *www.casadecolon.com*
- *Open 9am–6pm Mon–Fri, 10am–7pm Sat, 10am–3pm Sun*
- *Guided tours available on request*
- *Free*

Top 10 Features

1. Reproduction of *La Niña*
2. The Discovery
3. Canarian Emigration
4. Pre-Columbian Art
5. Early Navigation
6. 16th–20th-century Painting
7. Historical Las Palmas
8. Model and Maps of the Island
9. Ceilings and Courtyards
10. Façade

1 Reproduction of *La Niña*

Be transported back to the 15th century in this replica of *La Niña (below)*, said to have been Columbus's favourite ship. Of special note is the voyager's cabin, complete with a painting and crucifix from the original vessel.

2 The Discovery

Trace the four journeys Columbus made across the Atlantic on maps of his version of the world. A reproduction of his diary lies open at the page detailing his first stop in the Canary Islands, when he came ashore at Las Palmas and La Gomera before crossing the Atlantic into the unknown.

3 Canarian Emigration

Once the transatlantic route was established, Canarians emigrated in their hundreds. Paintings and information panels tell the story of the exodus and of the trades that thrived then failed.

4 Pre-Columbian Art

The high-ceilinged crypt contains some remarkable reproductions of Mexican and Ecuadorian pottery from 500 BC to the 10th century. Most are idols,while others are decorative pieces.

There's a market behind the museum on Sunday mornings.

5 Early Navigation

See absorbing old maps, atlases, and a globe from the year America was discovered. Trace the changing perceptions of the world from Ptolemy's sophisticated 2nd-century map through to increasingly accurate efforts in the 1500s.

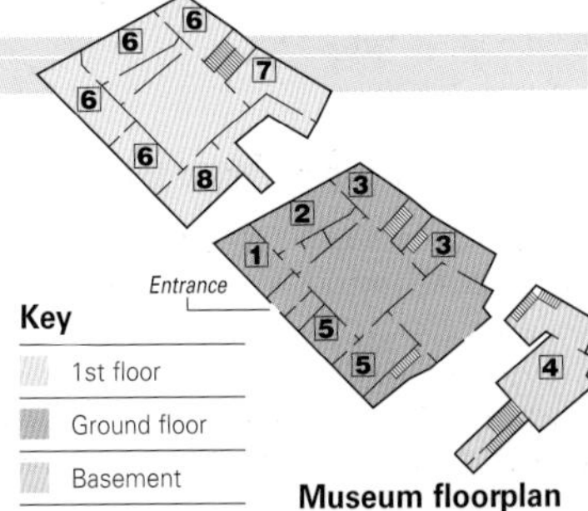

Museum floorplan

6 16th–20th-century Painting

A whistle-stop tour through 500 years of art starts with early religious paintings such as de Miranda's *Immaculada Concepcion (above)*. Visit the room dedicated to Canarian artists, with colourful 20th-century landscapes and a painting by local maestro Néstor de la Torre.

7 Historical Las Palmas

Children love the interactive model of late-17th-century Las Palmas. There are also models of the Castillo de la Luz *(below)* and Juan Rejón's original settlement of 1478.

8 Model and Maps of the Island

Plan your stay using a 3D model showing ravines, craters and mountains – a more up-to-date view of the island's topography.

9 Ceilings and Courtyards

The reproduction Mudéjar ceilings are very impressive. Upstairs, look heavenward for the only original section, ornately carved in dark wood. The second patio is also centuries old.

10 Façade

If you view the museum from the cobbled streets around it, you can spot details of Las Palmas's earliest architecture; parts of the façade date from the 1500s. However, the current building bears little resemblance to the original structure.

Love on the High Seas?

Some historians suggest that there was more on Columbus's mind than favourable winds and currents when he chose to pass through the Canaries. His decision to use La Gomera, rather than one of its larger, better-equipped neighbours, fuelled the suspicion that he was visiting his lover Beatriz de Bobadilla, a member of the Spanish court.

TOP 10 Catedral de Santa Ana, Las Palmas

Dominating the Vegueta skyline, the cathedral's twin bell towers are the most recognizable landmark of Las Palmas. Construction started just 14 years after the Spanish conquered Gran Canaria, but additions continued to be made late into the 19th century. The result is a microcosm of Canarian architecture: Gothic, Neo-Classical, Renaissance and local styles are all represented. Though this massive edifice differs wildly from the original, remnants of the 15th-century structure are still visible for those who care to track them down.

Neo-Classical façade, Catedral de Santa Ana

There are some lovely cafés and bars on nearly C/Mendizábal.

Entrance to the cathedral is via the Museo Diocesano de Arte Sacro on Calle Espíritu Santo. If you wish to attend mass, there are three daily Mon–Fri at 8:30am 9:15am and 7pm, and four daily Sat–Sun at 10am, noon, 1pm and 7pm.

- *C/Obispo Codina 13*
- *Map M5*
- *928 31 49 89*
- *Museo Diocesano de Arte Sacro: c/Espíritu Santo 20. Open 10am–4:30pm Mon–Fri, 10am–1:30pm Sat. Adm €3.00*

Top 10 Features

1. Museo Diocesano de Arte Sacro
2. Viewing Terrace
3. Façade
4. Chapels
5. Ceiling
6. Patio de los Naranjos
7. Sculptures
8. Paintings
9. Tombs
10. Square and Statues

1 Museo Diocesano de Arte Sacro

Adjoining the cathedral is a collection of religious art that includes sculptures, paintings and woodcarvings *(below)* dating back to the 16th century. Presiding over the Chaplain's Room is an important Luján Pérez crucifix. Sculpted in 1791, the crucifix leaves the confines of the cathedral once a year to appear in the city's Easter procession.

2 Viewing Terrace

Jump into the lift that whizzes you up to the cathedral's bell tower to enjoy fine views over the old town, commercial district and port *(right)*. A lively commentary sets the scene with a brief history of Las Palmas.

3 Façade

Aping the original Gothic design, the impressive Neo-Classical façade was added in the 19th century. From inside you can clearly see the join between the two.

4 Chapels

Fans of the morbid can see the preserved body of Bishop Buenaventura Codina in the Capilla de los Dolores. Of the other 10 chapels the Capilla de San Fernando stands out, with the cathedral's only Baroque altarpiece *(left)*.

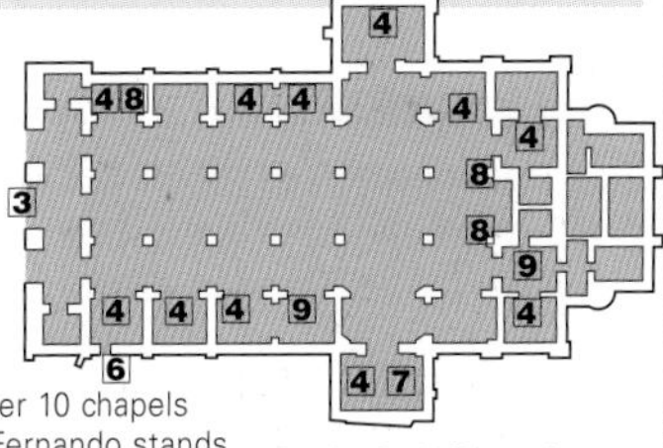

Cathedral floorplan

5 Ceiling

Crane your neck to admire the intricate Gothic ceiling. High above the altar, wooden statues of the apostles overlook the nave.

7 Sculptures

The cathedral's most significant sculpture is a Luján Pérez masterpiece, *Nuestra Señora de los Dolores* ("Our Lady of Sorrows") *(right)*, housed in the chapel of the same name. It accompanies the statue of Christ in the annual Easter parade. Also of note are the Baroque pulpits, and the 20th-century image of Santa Ana that guards the altar.

8 Paintings

Baroque paintings by Canarian maestro Juan de Miranda flank the altar. Juan de Roelas's elegant canvas in the Capilla de Santa Catalina is typical of 17th-century Sevillian art.

6 Patio de los Naranjos

Entered via the Puerta del Aire, this leafy 17th-century courtyard joins the cathedral to the Museum of Sacred Art. Built in typical Canarian manner, it is overlooked by carved wooden balconies.

9 Tombs

The grand tomb of ocal politician Fernando le León y Castillo, in he Capilla de Santa Teresa, was built by Miguel de la Torre in 1928. Historian and aturalist José de Viera y Clavijo, one-ime archdeacon of Fuerteventura, has a more modest omb in the Capilla le San José.

10 Square and Statues

Guarding the cathedral and the square in which it stands are eight statues depicting the dogs that supposedly gave the Canary Islands their name. Among the other grand buildings that line the large plaza are the episcopal palace and the old town hall.

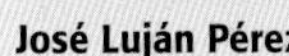

José Luján Pérez

Born in Santa María de Guía in 1756, Luján Pérez was Gran Canaria's most prolific and respected religious sculptor. Venerated for his ability to create perfectly-proportioned figures, he favoured sculptures of Christ or the Virgin Mary. Admire his intricate Baroque carvings in churches across the island, though his finest works are to be seen in its leading places of worship, the cathedral and the Basílica de Nuestra Señora del Pino in Teror *(see pp22–3)*.

TOP 10 Museo Canario, Las Palmas

Early Canarian history is a mysterious and fascinating subject that is given in-depth coverage in this excellent museum. The collection presents the most respected theories concerning the origins and practices of the Guanches, allowing you to reach your own conclusions. While most of the objects were unearthed on Gran Canaria, there is also detailed information on the primitive cultures of the other islands.

Façade, Museo Canario

The museum shop is located on the right hand side, just before you enter the museum. It sells handicrafts, books and souvenirs.

For those who want to delve deeper into Canarian history, the museum has a superlative library, which holds almost every book published in or about the Canary Islands, as well as a huge archive of Canarian newspapers dating back to 1879.

- *C/Dr Verneau 2*
- *Map L5*
- *928 33 68 00*
- *www.elmuseocanario.com*
- *Open 10am–8pm Mon–Fri, 10am–2pm Sat, Sun*
- *Admission €4.00 (concessions €2.40, children under 12 free)*

Top 10 Features

1. Housing
2. Pintaderas
3. Reproduction of the Cueva Pintada
4. Mummies
5. Aboriginal Ceramics
6. Funeral Rites and Medicine
7. Skulls and Bones
8. Agriculture and Farming
9. Magic and Religion
10. Traditional Pottery

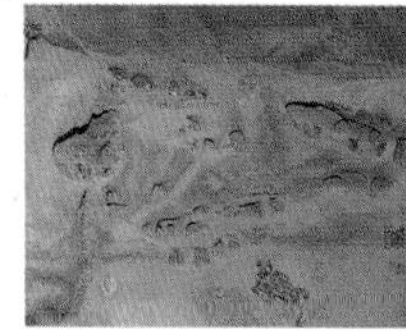

1 Housing

The Spaniards were intrigued to find primitive cave-dwellers living in artificial caves and stone houses alongside more advanced communities. Fascinating photos and models *(above)* illustrate both types of dwelling.

2 Pintaderas

The purpose of these small ceramic stamps *(below)* still isn't known. Guanches used them either to mark patterns on their skin or to personalize grain stores. Pick your own favourite and head to the museum shop for a replica necklace.

3 Reproduction of the Cueva Pintada

The original site is in Gáldar but you can also see some Guanche art at the museum. The geometric patterns *(above)* in black, white and red represent the finest examples of cave art to be seen on the islands. The museum's version is an almost perfect replica of the original.

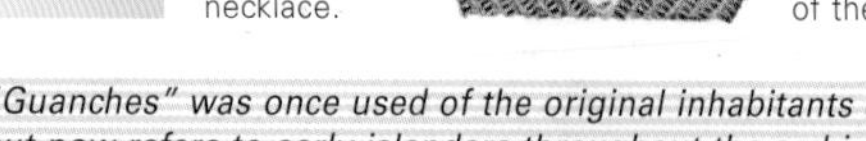

"Guanches" was once used of the original inhabitants of Tenerife, but now refers to early islanders throughout the archipelago.

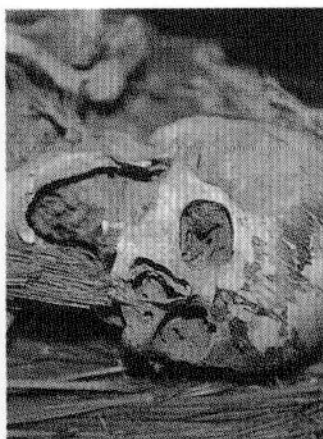

4 Mummies

Some theories link the Guanches to the Egyptians, due to their similar methods of mummification. Archeologists continue to uncover artifacts across the archipelago, but the tombs were raided long ago and their contents sold to the museum, where you can see various mummies on display.

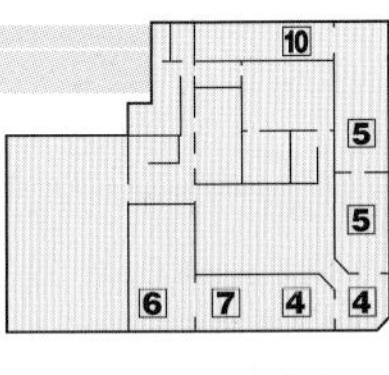

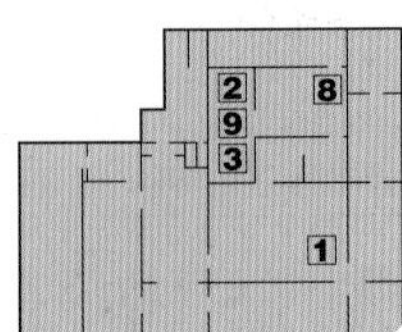

Museum floorplan

Key

1st Floor

Ground Floor

5 Aboriginal Ceramics

This island-by-island showcase of aboriginal ceramics also includes the primitive tools used to create them.

6 Funeral Rites and Medicine

With mummification reserved for the higher classes, the Guanches also built stone tombs and rickety wooden coffins. Ghoulish skulls illustrate trepanation, a medical procedure in which cranial holes were drilled to ease pain.

7 Skulls and Bones

Hundreds of smiling skulls adorn the walls in this eerie yet intriguing room *(above)*. Debate continues to rage as to whether the remains are of Cro-Magnon man.

8 Agriculture and Farming

The basic tools on display demonstrate the tough life of the pastoral Guanches, who survived on limited resources.

9 Magic and Religion

Chroniclers of the Conquest wrote that the Guanches worshipped a single god, but the survival of numerous idols suggests this was not the case. Most deities found on the island take the female form; the largest, the Tara Idol *(below)*, is now a symbol of pride for Canary Islanders.

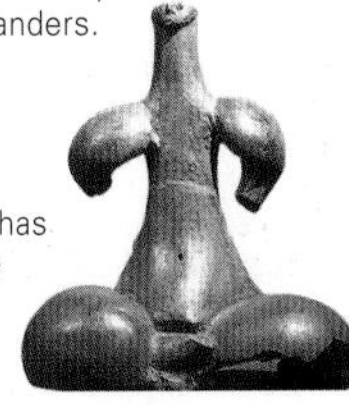

10 Traditional Pottery

The tradition of crafting pottery without using a wheel has persisted on Gran Canaria. See some examples, and find out where to go if you're after an almost authentic Guanche pot.

Like Canaries and Dogs

Early inhabitants called the island Tamarán. When the conquerors arrived, they split it into two cantons, each led by a *guanarteme* (chief). Outsiders have referred to the island as Canaria for at least 2,000 years, though few can agree whether it was named after dogs, birds or the Berber tribe – the Canarii – who may have inhabited it.

Jardín Botánico Viera y Clavijo

Nestled in the Guiniguada ravine, Spain's largest botanical garden in Tafira Alta, is 7 km (4 miles) from Las Palmas. Its steep paths are cloaked in Macronesian flora, both endemic and imported. You by no means have to be a botanist to enjoy the garden as it's a peaceful place for a stroll, a respite from the hustle and bustle of the capital. Although pretty in any season, the best time to visit is in January or February, after the winter rains have worked their magic.

Cactuses, Jardín Botánico Viera y Clavijo

If the garden's superb restaurant *(see p60)* is too pricey, there are several cheaper eateries near the lower entrance.

The garden has two entrances. One is on the GC310 (lower entrance), the other on the GC110 (upper entrance). Disabled visitors are advised to enter by the lower gate; although much of the garden isn't accessible, the lower section is step-free.

- *GC310 & GC110*
- *Map E2*
- *928 21 95 80*
- *www.jardincanario.org*
- *8am–6pm daily*
- *Free*
- *Limited disabled access from entrance on GC310*
- *Exhibition Centre: 8am–2:30pm Mon–Fri*

Top 10 Features

1. Plaza de Viera y Clavijo
2. Laurel Forest
3. Pine Wood
4. Islands Garden
5. Cactuses and Succulents
6. Stone Bridge
7. El Alpendre
8. Exhibition Centre
9. Fountain of the Wise
10. Plaza Matias Vega

1 Plaza de Viera y Clavijo

The first port of call for those using the upper entrance is this small square, overlooked by a bust of 18th-century historian and naturalist José de Viera y Clavijo. The view of the gardens from here *(below)* gives a sneak preview of what's in store.

2 Laurel Forest

Until the last ice age, much of Europe was covered in laurel forest *(laurisilva)*; the only survi-ving examples are in the Canary Islands and Madeira. A small area of the garden was planted with *laurisilva* in 1964. Within it are some rare species, including the Garoé tree, sacred to the original inhabitants of El Hierro.

3 Pine Wood

If you don't get time to visit a natural Canarian pine forest, at least breathe in the fresh scent of pine trees here. In spring, look out for the bright blossoms of the Canary gum and foxglove.

4 Islands Garden

Get an overview of the plant life of all seven islands, including some rare species. The plants are grouped by island of origin *(below)*.

Stock up on aloe vera products at the kiosk in Plaza Matías Vega, open 10am–2pm, 3–6pm Mon–Fri.

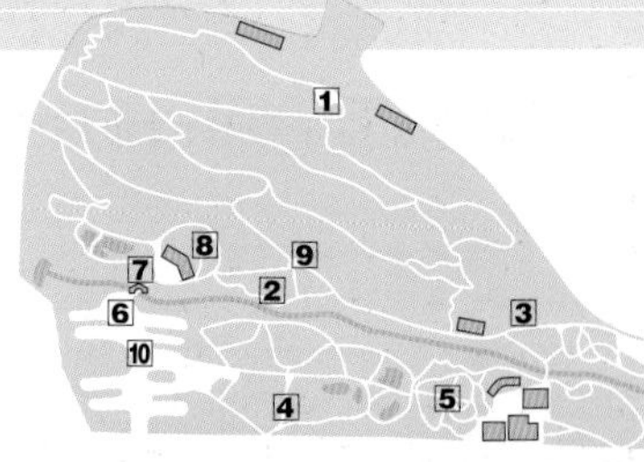

Plan of Jardín Botánico Viera y Clavijo

5 Cactuses and Succulents

The lowest part of the garden is home to an impressive array of cactuses, of both native and imported species. There are around 2,000 varieties of succulent plant on display in this section of the botanical garden, almost a third of the world's known species.

6 Stone Bridge

The busy road that separates the Vegueta and Triana districts in Las Palmas runs through what was once a lush ravine – part of the same ravine that traverses the garden. The stone bridge that crosses it *(above)* is a replica of that which once linked the capital's oldest neighbourhoods.

7 El Alpendre

Built in traditional Canarian style, this stone farm shed predates the surrounding gardens. It was restored in 1989 and holds a thresher, silo, plough and other articles used in local agriculture.

9 Fountain of the Wise

This basalt monument *(above)* pays tribute to important local botanists. A panel lists plant species beside the discoverers who named them.

8 Exhibition Centre

If you want to delve deeper into the world of Canarian flora, the small exhibition centre has detailed information on the many habitats found on the Canary Islands. Audio-visual and interactive exhibits add to the information provided in the wall displays.

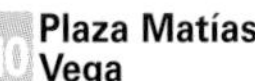

10 Plaza Matías Vega

Beside the lower entrance, this square is surrounded by one of the archipelago's most emblematic plants, the Canarian palm tree *(Phoenix canariensis)*. On La Gomera, the sap from this tree is used to make a type of honey.

Roots and Branches

Swedish botanist Eric Sventenius set up the garden in 1952, aiming to create a space where people could enjoy plants from across the islands without needing to get on a boat. After the death of Sventenius in 1972, British naturalist David Bramwell took over the reins, and developed the garden as an investigative centre as well as a public park. Today it has an international reputation as a conservation and research centre, conducting important studies into the unique Canarian flora.

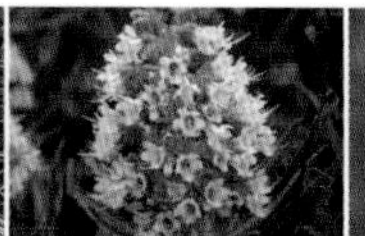

Left **Canary Island pine** Middle **Viper's bugloss** Right **Canary Island bellflower**

TOP 10 Gran Canarian Plants

1 Gran Canaria Dragon Tree

A subspecies of the legendary dragon tree *(Dracaena tamaranae)* was discovered on Gran Canaria in 1972. With just 20 known examples, it is one of the rarest trees in the world. Despite its thinner, more pointed leaves, it strongly resembles the common dragon tree, and shares its renowned red sap, known as "dragon's blood".

2 Foxglove

A sighting of these endemic copper- or deep-red-coloured flowers *(Isoplexis chalcantha, Isoplexis isabelliana)* is a treat, since they are now so rare. Two species of foxglove exist on the island, one thriving in highlands and pine forests, and the other struggling to survive in the depleted laurel forest.

3 Canary Island Spurge

This cactus-like plant *(Euphorbia canariensis)* is widespread throughout the island, but no less impressive for that. Resembling a giant candlestick, it favours arid zones such as lava fields and rocky cliffs. The milky sap of the plant is poisonous to humans.

Canary Island date palms

4 Viper's Bugloss

These conical flowers are a common yet attractive sight across the islands. Gran Canaria viper's bugloss *(Echium decaisnei)* is abundant, but the vivid blue Tenteniguada viper's bugloss *(Echium callithyrsum)* grows only in the northern highlands of the isle.

5 Gran Canaria Tansy

A big hit with gardeners everywhere, this white-and-yellow daisy-like flower is unique to Gran Canaria. It is quite common in low inland areas, although you might also spot a few on the higher peaks.

6 Canary Island Bellflower

You're likely to see this pretty orange flower *(Canarina canariensis)* if you take the time to explore the island's northern laurel forest, Los Tilos de Moya.

7 Canary Island Date Palm

Found only on the archipelago and present on all seven islands, this species of palm tree *(Phoenix canariensis)* is now the official botanical emblem of the Canaries. Found in low-lying, warm valleys, it is an attractive feature of the landscape, as well as a valuable resource used in construction, handicrafts and even for making foodstuffs.

The first dragon tree is said to have grown on the spot where Hercules slayed the dragon Ladon – hence its "legendary" status.

8 Canary Island Pine

A relic of Mediterranean flora from the Tertiary Era, Gran Canaria's pine forests are among the finest on the archipelago. Restricted to areas above 600m (1,968 ft), Canary Island pine *(Pinus canariensis)* is unique to the islands, and its wood has long been utilized in construction, thanks to its strength.

9 Sea Lavender

Those who like a challenge should look out for this elegant flower *(Limonium sventenii)*, exclusive to Gran Canaria. The plant, which can grow up to one metre (3 ft) tall, is crowned with clusters of bright blue or violet flowers. Keep an eye out for it on the northwestern cliffs and on the island's mountains.

10 Houseleek

Popular with gardeners worldwide, houseleeks are something of a Canarian motif. Their attractive rosette-shaped leaves can be seen protruding from rock faces across the island. The most striking examples are the *Aeonium manriqueorum* and *Aeonium percarneum,* both boasting attractive blooms.

Top 10 Exotic Plants

1. Jacaranda
2. Rutya Fruicosa
3. Aloe Vera
4. Lotus Kunkeli
5. Yucca
6. Queen's Wreath
7. Parolinia Glabriuscul
8. Poinsettia
9. Bird of paradise
10. Queen Palm

The Lost World of Canarian Flora

Even the most world-weary traveller will be impressed by the wealth of the Canary Islands' flora. The diversity is exceptional, with more than 500 unique plant species, many of which are survivors from the Ice Age. Species long-extinct elsewhere thrive here and some even look prehistoric, while imported species bloom alongside Canarian and Macronesian plants. In little over an hour you can drive from the arid coast, through misty laurel forest and up to pine forests scattered across the highest peaks.

Bird of paradise
Up to one metre (3 ft) tall, this plant flourishes in tropical climates worldwide. Its splendid flower boasts bright orange and brilliant blue "tongues".

Dragon tree

April to May is the best time to spot flora on the island.

TOP 10 Maspalomas

Maspalomas is best known for its magnificent sand dunes, protected as a nature reserve. Part of the original expanse was destroyed in a flurry of construction in the 1960s and 1970s; many plant and animal species were lost at that time, but the authorities are working to reintroduce them. Today Maspalomas is one of the Canary Islands' largest resorts, but it's still easy to find a peaceful spot in which to enjoy the sun away from the tourist crowds.

Maspalomas's distinctive 19th-century lighthouse

Small kiosks called *chiringuitos* sell sandwiches and beer and are dotted around the beach. Or take a picnic and eat lunch on a bench next to the lagoon, where you can look out for bird life.

Walk through the dunes in the early morning or late evening to avoid burning your feet.

- *Map D6*
- *Information centre: open 8am–2:30pm Mon–Fri, 928 765 242*
- *Golf green fees: €60.00 (summer), €105.00 (winter)*
- *Camel rides: 9am–4pm daily. €12.00 (adults), €8.00 (children); Camello Safari Dunas, 928 76 07 81; Camel Safari Park La Baranda, 928 79 86 80*

Top 10 Features

1. Sand Dunes
2. Information Centre
3. Maspalomas Beach
4. Lagoon and Palm Grove
5. Bird-watching
6. Lighthouse
7. Golf Course
8. Camel Rides
9. Mirador
10. The Resort

1 Sand Dunes

Contrary to popular belief, these 400 ha (988 acres) of golden sand *(right)* didn't blow across from the nearby Sahara Desert; they washed up from the ocean. While a large part is constantly on the move, there is also a stable section, home to a variety of flora and bird life. Stick to the signed routes to protect the ecosystem.

2 Information Centre

The small information centre explains the origins of the dunes, and the plant and animal life you can expect to spot. Find out about the conservation efforts and environmental problems, or arrange to join a guided walk.

3 Maspalomas Beach

This *(below)* is Gran Canaria's supreme beach. Families favour the calmer seas near the lighthouse. The section closest to Playa del Inglés is used by nudists.

4 Lagoon and Palm Grove

A few palm trees and date palms remain of a grove all but destroyed by construction. Keep an eye out for mullet, guppies and bream in the murky waters of the small lagoon alongside it.

Be aware that the dunes are a renowned cruising area for gay men.

5 Bird-watching

As well as local species, a wealth of migrating birds use the site as a pit stop. In spring and autumn look out for kingfisher, heron, curlew and egret, along with the usual nesting birds – kestrel, plover and moorhen. Less common species include osprey, courser and grey duck, all of which came close to being wiped out here by man's activities.

Maspalomas

6 Lighthouse

Standing in a square lined with palm trees is one of the island's most striking landmarks. The 55-m (180-ft) lighthouse was built in the late 19th century by local engineer Juan de León y Castillo.

7 Golf Course

Unrivalled weather and vistas of the dunes and ocean beyond make Maspalomas's golf course *(above)* special. Non-members are welcome to tee off here.

8 Camel Rides

Pretend you really are in the desert as you ride through the dunes on the back of a dromedary. Trips leave from the east side of the ravine, just to the north of the lagoon. A half-hour ride takes you through areas thick with daisies and tamarisk, and is one way to avoid burning your feet.

9 Mirador

You'll get a fine view and some super snaps from the *mirador,* or viewing point, near the information centre. This is where the nature walks through the dunes start.

10 The Resort

The area is still best known as a major tourist resort favoured by northern Europeans. Maspalomas was a victim of the construction boom but it is a far more exclusive resort than its raucous, party-all-night neighbour Playa del Inglés.

Conservation, not Construction

Today, local government is attempting to repair the havoc wreaked by mass construction, with schemes to reintroduce bird and plant species once common in the area. Not so long ago, the priority was to profit from the dunes at all costs, even if it meant giving planning approval to projects that would inevitably damage the fragile ecosystem. The demolition of a half-built hotel in the dunes in 1989 was a turning point in saving Gran Canaria's most notable landscape from total destruction.

TOP 10 Teror

A visit to Teror is a must, not only for its exquisite Canarian architecture, but also because of its historic and religious importance. An independent parish since 1514, Teror is one of the oldest urban centres on the island. Its religious connections date back to the time when the Virgin Mary was sighted under a pine tree in a nearby forest. The Madonna of the Pine later became the island's patron saint, and pilgrims travel from near and far to pay homage and bring gifts. The wonderful town centre was declared a heritage sight in 1979.

C/Real de la Plaza, Teror

Popular locally, El Rincón de Magüi (C/ Diputación 6) offers good Canarian food.

Behind the basilica is an excellent tourist information office.

- *Map D2*
- *Tourist information office: open 9am–4:30pm Mon–Fri*
- *Basílica de Nuestra Señora del Pino: Open 1–8pm Mon, 9am–1pm, 3–8pm Tue–Fri, 9am–8:30pm Sat, 7am–7:30pm Sun*
- *Casa Museo de los Patronos de la Virgen: Plaza de Nuestra Señora del Pino. Open 11am–4pm Mon–Fri, 10am–2pm Sat–Sun. Adm €3.00. Disabled access only to lower floor*
- *Market: 9am–3pm Sun*
- *Cistercian Convent: C/Obispo Pozuelo. Open 10am–1pm, 4–6pm daily (for sale of cakes and biscuits only)*
- *Finca de Osorio: GC43, around 2km (just over a mile) from Teror. 928 630 090. Open 9am–5pm daily; visits by appointment only. Free*

Top 10 Features

1. Basílica de Nuestra Señora del Pino
2. Casa de los Patronos de la Virgen
3. Calle Real de la Plaza
4. Fiesta del Pino
5. Market
6. Cistercian Convent
7. Finca de Osorio
8. Chorizo de Teror
9. Casa de Cultura
10. Plaza Teresa de Bolivar

1 Basílica de Nuestra Señora del Pino

Home to the Madonna of the Pine, this is perhaps the most religiously significant building on the island *(above)*.

2 Casa de los Patronos de la Virgen

Teror's main museum offers a glimpse into how the Canarian gentry lived in years gone by. Delightfully furnished rooms *(right)* and a small chapel encircle the patio, which has an Italian fountain as its centrepiece. Authentic, right down to the musty smell that still lingers.

3 Calle Real de la Plaza

Those who appreciate Canarian architecture will love this peaceful street, with its traditional wooden balconies and red-tiled roofs.

4 Fiesta del Pino

On 8 September each year, Teror transforms from a sleepy parish into a hive of activity. Pilgrims walk from all over the island to join in the festivities in honour of their patron saint *(above)*.

For more on the Basílica de Nuestra Señora del Pino **See pp22–3**

5 Market

Gran Canaria's oldest market offers a curious blend of traditional foodstuffs, bric-a-brac and religious memorabilia. The stall-holders set up behind the church on Sundays, bringing a feeling of life to the otherwise eerily quiet town.

6 Cistercian Convent

The nuns at this convent sell home-made cakes. Ring the bell and a turntable will rotate showing what's on offer. Place your money on the turn-table and voice your preference. An unseen nun will pass your cakes and change.

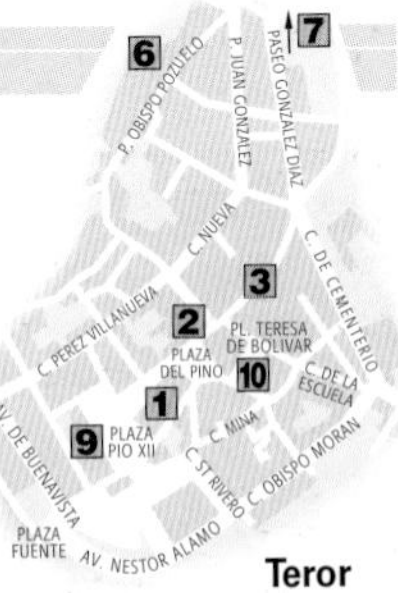

Teror

7 Finca de Osorio

Located in the lush Parque Rural de Doramas, this farm boasts some unique flora, such as the pretty Canarian bellflower. Other highlights include shrew, owl and fine views from Pico de Osorio.

8 Chorizo de Teror

Garlic lovers will adore the local sandwich-filler *(above)*. This flavour-some spreadable sausage is available at every bar and restaurant, and also at the Sunday market.

9 Casa de la Cultura (Episcopal Palace)

Part of this magnificent building *(below)* is still home to the bishop, but a large section is used for temporary exhibitions by local artists. This is fitting as it was the townsfolk who presented the house to the Canarian bishops in the 18th century, in gratitude for their support in building the basilica.

10 Plaza Teresa de Bolívar

Built in 1953 as an over-spill for the Fiesta del Pino, this square *(above)* was dedicated to Teresa de Bolívar, wife of the South American revolutionary Simón Bolívar. Her family hailed from Teror, and the family crest adorns the square.

The Green Heart of Gran Canaria

Although best known for its architecture, Teror also boasts some areas of supreme natural beauty, which have earned it the title *el corazón verde de Gran Canaria* ("the green heart of Gran Canaria"). Thanks to considerable winter rainfall, the region has lush ravines, palm groves and an area of rare laurel forest. Above the town, the Caldera de Pino Santo (Holy Pine Crater) and its environs have been declared a protected landscape in recognition of their natural beauty.

Left **Stained-glass windows** Middle **The façade of the basilica** Right **Christ tied to a column**

TOP 10 Basílica de Nuestra Señora del Pino

1 Nuestra Señora del Pino

For hundreds of years, the faithful have embroidered the flamboyant cloaks that adorn the Virgin *(see p20)*. Beneath the gowns stands a wooden Gothic sculpture from the late 1500s or early 1600s. The theft in 1975 of a selection of precious stones from her crown is still a sore point among locals. For a close look at the statue, enter through the basilica's *camarín*.

2 Main Altarpiece

Ornately carved from dark wood, the main altarpiece is the work of Nicolás Jacinto, and is considered the finest example of Rococo art on the island. Crowned with the Virgin's ornate silver throne, and with a glorious silver frontispiece decorating its lower section, it outshines all its competitors.

3 Treasure Room

This is where you can really get to grips with the importance the Madonna has for the people of the island. The room contains a bizarre selection of gifts donated by the faithful, including trophies and medals, notes and coins from around the world, and a plethora of football memorabilia signed by the island's various teams. An adjoining room showcases the Virgin's many outfits, some of which date back to the 18th century. She dons a different dress each year during the Fiestas del Pino.

4 Christ tied to a column

The main focus of Teror's Easter parades is an anguished statue carved by maestro Luján Pérez in 1793. Considered one of his finest works, the image is flanked by statues of St Michael and the Resurrection, also from the late 18th century.

The Crucified

5 *The Crucified*

This eerily lit image of Christ on the cross is another Luján Pérez piece, dating back to 1790 – among the finest that he produced.

6 Other Statues

Other noteworthy sculptures in the basilica include a marvellous image of St Matthew clutching a crucifix, and a flamboyant gold-plated image of St Ramón Nonato. The most recent statue is *The Sacred Heart of Jesus,* which dates from the early years of the 20th century.

The Basilica's telephone number is 928 61 34 28. For its opening times **See p20**

7 Stained-glass Windows
Amongst the finest examples is an image of Pope Pius X from 1914, when the Virgin of the Pine was named Gran Canaria's patron saint. The window is on the main façade, along with an impressive image of Pope Pius XII, commemorated for his visit here.

8 Altar of Souls
The least flamboyant of the church's altars is perhaps also its most striking, with its weathered painting of souls anguishing in Purgatory.

9 The Building
Little remains of the previous churches erected on this site. The octagonal tower was a feature of the 17th-century building; the present (1767) tower is a replica.

10 Rescued Relics
Two relics remain from previous incarnations of the church: a large stone font from the first, 16th–century chapel, now in the *camarín;* and, in the treasure room, a cross fashioned from the pine tree where the vision of the Virgin was first seen.

Top 10 Bizarre Gifts to the Madonna

1. Football signed by the Las Palmas team
2. Broken watch
3. British pound note with message asking for help
4. Toy car
5. Sports trophies
6. Academic certificates
7. Well–loved teddy
8. Garish souvenir–style statuettes
9. Specially composed poems
10. Military medals

The Holiest Statue

On 8 September 1481, the Virgin Mary appeared to Juan Frías, bishop of Gran Canaria, in the branches of a pine tree. He could never have guessed how venerated that image of her would become. A statue of the Madonna was enshrined in a small church in the centre of Teror. Since then, the devoted have revered Nuestra Señora del Pino (Our Lady of the Pine). The original church has been replaced twice, and has gradually grown into the huge edifice we see today. It is an important site for pilgrims wishing to worship the Virgin, and there is an annual two-day festival combining religious devotion with earthly fun. This culminates in an evening procession on 8 September in which locals offer fresh produce to their patron saint.

Nuestra Señora del Pino

The camarín (for access to the treasure room and Madonna) is open 1–3pm daily.

TOP 10 La Cumbre

La Cumbre – "the Summit" – is the mountainous heart of the island. Worlds away from the sun-and-sand image of the Canaries, Gran Canaria's highest peaks are often shrouded in mist, and snow is not unusual in winter. The two most recognizable rocks, Nublo and Bentayga, were considered holy ground by the Guanches. Now sparsely populated, the region has maintained local traditions more than any other part of the island. Enjoy some unrivalled vistas and hearty food – and don't miss the aboriginal homes and places of worship

View from the Mirador Degollada de la Becerra

Enjoy a picnic in the mountains at one of the *cabildo* (local government) sites. The best are Llanos de la Pez and Llanos de Ana López, both on the GC600. You can also camp here, as long as you get permission.

- *Map C3, D3*

Top 10 Features

1. Roque Nublo
2. Roque Bentayga
3. Cuevas del Rey
4. El Fraile and La Rana
5. Tejeda
6. Pico de las Nieves
7. Mirador Degollada de la Becerra
8. Artenara
9. Cruz de Tejeda
10. Hiking and Climbing

1 Roque Nublo

The Canaries' most famous rock *(right)* is part of a volcanic chimney. Follow the path from the road to the "Cloud Rock", or snap it from anywhere in the interior.

2 Roque Bentayga

Transport yourself to the Stone Age by exploring this pre-Hispanic site *(above)*. Offerings and sacrifices were probably made here.

3 Cuevas del Rey

Hollowed out of the west face of Bentayga, no one knows if the man-made "Caves of the King" *(right)* were used by monarchs. The largest cave is known as Cueva del Guayre.

4 El Fraile and La Rana

With a bit of imagination, two of Roque Nublo's neighbours become more than just rocks. Viewed from the GC60 near Ayacata, El Fraile ("The Friar") does resemble a monk in prayer. Making a frog out of La Rana, the monolith closest to Roque Nublo, requires a little more effort.

Map of La Cumbre

5 Tejeda

Satisfy your sweet tooth at Tejeda with ɔme traditional almond delicacies, or view cal sculpture in the Museo de Abraham árdenes. In February, a series of fiestas ıarks the blossoming of the almond trees.

6 Pico de las Nieves

The view from this peak of 1,949 m (6,394 ft) is marred by the presence of a military radio station, but on a clear day you'll still enjoy fine panoramas across the central mountains down to the coast.

7 Mirador Degollada de la Becerra

ews don't get any ɜtter; from here you ·n see Roque Nublo, ɔque Bentayga and, on ear days, Spain's ghest peak, ount Teide ı Tenerife.

8 Artenara

Cave culture rules in Gran Canaria's highest and chilliest town. Look around the simple 19th-century church, enjoy the remarkable views, and pay a visit to the cave-chapel before a warming lunch.

9 Cruz de Tejeda

l roads lead to ·uz de Tejeda, e large stone oss at the and's central point, here there are ɔnkey rides, two ıperb restaurants ıd a splendid Parador.

10 Hiking and Climbing

Hikers can choose from three treks of varying lengths and levels. The three-hour circuit from La Culata is outstanding, if a little strenuous. Adrenaline-junkies relish the climb up the 80-m (260-ft) Roque Nublo.

Explosion and Erosion

The rugged landscape of central Gran Canaria wasn't created overnight. Millions of years of explosive eruptions and erosion gave rise to the awe-inspiring Caldera de Tejeda. It's one of the oldest parts of the island; volcanic activity was at its height here around 10 million years ago. After a particularly violent explosion, the centre of the volcano sank, leaving a crater 18 km (11 miles) wide. The emblematic rocks crowning the crater are the result of five million years of erosion.

For more on the Cruz de Tejeda **See p82**

Top 10 Caldera de Bandama

The Guanches considered this crater of an extinct volcano a fine place to live. When Dutch businessman Daniel Van Damme visited in the early 16th century he spotted the fertile land's potential and planted vines here. Grateful for the tip, locals named the gaping hole after the Dutchman. The perfectly formed crater covers 326 ha (806 acres), and gained protected status in 1994. Often overlooked by locals and tourists alike, it's a stunning sight and a wonderful place for spotting native flora, or just enjoying the utter silence.

Hiking path in the Caldera de Bandama

In the cluster of houses on the road to La Atalaya, there's a nameless, family-run bar. Sample cheap traditional favourites here.

The road to the peak is closed from 10pm–8am daily.

- *Map E3*
- *Bandama Golf Hotel: 928 351 538. www.bandamagolfhotel.com*
- *Real Club de Golf: Ctra de Bandama s/n, Sta Brígida. 928 35 01 04. www.realclubdegolfdelaspalmas.com*
- *Casa del Vino de Gran Canaria: El Galeón, Calle Calvo Sotelo 26, Sta Brígida. 928 64 48 84. Open 10am–2pm Tue–Sun.*

Top 10 Sights

1. Caldera
2. Flora
3. Disused Buildings
4. Vistas
5. Hiking
6. Golf
7. Wine
8. Cuevas de los Canarios
9. Restaurant
10. Bandama Golf Hotel

1 Caldera

With a diameter of 800 m (2,600 ft) and an average depth of 200 m (650 ft), Bandama is the largest recent crater on the island. Details of the last eruption remain vague, but vulcanologists agree that Bandama expelled its fiery heart once and for all over 5,000 years ago.

2 Flora

The crater is a haven for endemic flora. As well as cactuses and palm trees, look out for white viper's bugloss, olive and mastic trees, and some impressive houseleeks.

3 Disused Buildings

A threshing floor and a wine press dating back to the 18th century are among the abandoned structures within the crater. Nearby, there's the rather more recent home of a hardy farmer who has lived here for many years.

4 Vistas

A spiralling road takes you to the peak, 574 m (1,883 ft) above sea level, from where you can enjoy a stunning panorama of Gran Canaria *(below)*. The view highlights the island's diversity, encompassing as it does the bustling cities of Telde and Las Palmas, the varied east coast beaches and the high central peaks.

5 Hiking

There's no better ·ay to experience andama than by ·iking to the crater oor. A clear path ·ads down from ehind the bar on the ·oad to La Atalaya. At ·e bottom, there is a ·rcular walk around ·e crater's interior.

8 Cuevas de los Canarios

hose with a head for eights should visit the ·uanche caves inside the rater *(above)*. These ·an-made grottos house wellings, an extensive rain store and unique ·ock engravings. To reach ·em, follow the start of ·e hiking route but take ·e path to your left after ·aving the cobbled road.

9 Restaurant

Perched precariously on the north face of the mountain is a restaurant serving local and international cuisine. The view of Las Palmas is unrivalled.

10 Bandama Golf Hotel

With fine views of the crater, the hotel *(below)* is perfectly situated for a relaxing break. Rooms are simple but cosy.

6 Golf

Play a few holes at the Real Club de Golf *(left)*, Spain's oldest golf club. Founded in 1891, the par-71 course enjoys a fine location and is open to non-members only on weekday mornings.

7 Wine

Since the last eruption took place, the soil here has been ideal for vines. Today the area is the focal point of the island's wine route, with five *bodegas* lining the approach road to the crater. Some have the *denominación de origen* seal of quality, while others produce less sophisticated vintages. To sample or purchase wine visit the Casa del Vino (Wine Museum).

Volcanic Farming

Setting up home in the bottom of a volcanic crater may seem like a strange idea, and hoping to farm the land even stranger. The fact, though, is that this environment provides the perfect conditions for cultivation, particularly of vines. Loose stones, known locally as *picón*, trap moisture during the night and release it when the sun shines. Daniel Van Damme soon worked this out, and his method of covering plants with volcanic stones is still practised today by the crater's only inhabitant.

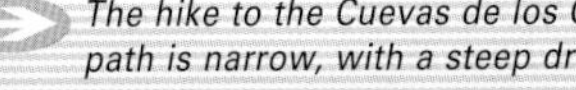

The hike to the Cuevas de los Canarios isn't difficult, but the path is narrow, with a steep drop. Avoid in wet conditions.

Top 10 Barranco de Guayadeque

Deep ravines, carving great chunks out of the landscape, are characteristic of Gran Canaria, but none of them is more impressive than the Barranco de Guayadeque (which in the Guanche language means "place of running water"). In addition to its great natural beauty, this fascinating area has an important cultural heritage, and harbours unique flora and fauna. The small local troglodyte population dwells in cave-homes and strives to maintain a way of life that has been lost elsewhere on the island.

Montaña de las Tierras, Barranco de Guayadeque

If you fancy tasting traditional Canarian cuisine, Guayadeque is a fine place to start. In keeping with the local theme, the restaurants are based in man-made caves scattered along the ravine, with chairs and tables carved out of the rock. The best eateries are in Montaña de las Tierras. Visit midweek to avoid the crowds competing for tables.

Allow a full day to explore the ravine properly.

- *Map E4*
- *GC103 from Agüimes or GC122 from Ingenio*
- *Museo de Guayadeque: 928 17 20 26. Open 9am–5pm Tue–Sat, 10am–3pm Sun. Adm €2.50 (children under 12, €1)*

Top 10 Features

1. Museo de Guayadeque
2. Guanche Settlements
3. Ermita de San Bartolomé de Guayadeque
4. Troglodyte Village (Cuevas Bermejas)
5. Picnics and Barbecues
6. Cave Restaurants
7. Montaña de las Tierras
8. Hiking
9. Flora and Fauna
10. Views

1 Museo de Guayadeque

Based in a cave, this museum offers an insight into life in the ravine, from the Guanches to the present-day troglodytes. There is information on mummification, farming, the rare flora to be found in the ravine, and even how to build a cave home.

2 Guanche Settlements

Densely inhabited before the Conquest *(see p34)*, the Barranco de Guayadeque is littered with caves, both natural and man-made. The finest, Cuevas Muchas, contains houses, a grain store, and burial sites.

3 Ermita de San Bartolomé de Guayadeque

Apart from the pews, everything in Guayadeque's cave chapel *(left)*, situated in Cuevas Bermejas, is carved out of the rock. When the hermitage was set up is not known, but the crucifix appears to date from just after the Conquest

Beware – Cuevas Muchas is high up in the ravine and dangerous to visit; it's best viewed from the safety of the road.

4 Troglodyte Village (Cuevas Bermejas)

hough the tradition of etting up home in a ave has survived, these 1st-century troglodyte bodes have little to do vith their pre-Conquest ounterparts. A peek hrough an open door is kely to reveal a television nd even a fitted kitchen.

5 Picnics and Barbecues

If you wish to admire the ravine's natural beauty as you eat, take your own food and enjoy a picnic. There are also areas set up for barbecues *(above)* so, if you fancy one, buy some charcoal and sausages and join the locals.

6 Cave Restaurants

Hearty traditional Canarian dishes such as vegetable stew, goat and *gofio* *(see p61)* are on the menu at most of the local eateries *(below)*, but the real appeal is the setting, not the cuisine.

7 Montaña de las Tierras

The road comes to an abrupt halt at this small farming village *(above)*. Follow the cobbled path from here for a tour of rural Gran Canaria. Four-wheel-drive vehicles can continue along the dirt track, but it's too rough for normal cars.

8 Hiking

Hikers rule in the upper section of the ravine, where the road fizzles out. The finest of several short walks skirts the Caldera de los Marteles. Ask in the museum for a walks map.

9 Flora and Fauna

Among 80 species of flora, there are two plants found nowhere else in the world. Reptiles are abundant, and you might spot the island's only native mammal, a species of bat.

10 Views

The lookout point situated in Montaña de las Tierras provides a good view of the lower part of the ravine *(left)*, though the best vistas are from the GC120 from Ingenio to Cuevas Blancas.

A Language Lost

Little has survived of the Guanche language – a mere smattering of words such as *baifo* (kid's meat) and *gofio* (roasted corn or barley). One thing you'll notice, though, is the abundance of unusual place-names on the island, most with a distinctly non-Spanish sound. Artenara, Agaete, Arguineguin, Tocodoman and Tenteniguada are amongst the multitude of names whose origins predate the Conquest. Alas, most of their meanings are lost; one of the few exceptions is Guayadeque.

Top 10 Puerto de las Nieves

Puerto de las Nieves – the "Port of the Snows" – was once the island's principal port, but it suffered a blow in the 19th century with the construction of Puerto de la Luz in Las Palmas. The lack of major maritime traffic has allowed the enchanting harbour, with its uniform low, white-and-blue houses, to retain its charm. Today it is important as the main departure point for Tenerife. Hundreds of visitors pass through the village, but it merits more than a cursory glance through the bus window en route to the ferry.

View of the port, Puerto de las Nieves

Don't forget to sample the local brew – strong coffee grown in the nearby Agaete valley.

If possible visit mid-week, as it's a popular spot for daytripping locals at weekends.

- *Map B2*
- *Ermita de las Nieves. 928 89 82 62. Open 11am–1pm Mon–Sat, 9–11am Sun*

Top 10 Features

1. Dedo de Dios
2. Ermita de las Nieves
3. Bajada de la Rama
4. Beach
5. Ferries to Tenerife
6. Seafood Restaurants
7. Fishing
8. Old Relics
9. Reproduction of Maipés de Abajo
10. Diving and Surfing

1 Dedo de Dios

The curious basaltic monolith known as the "Finger of God" was destroyed in 2005 by a tropical storm. Despite the fact that it no longer exists, it is still the emblem of the village.

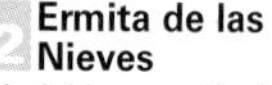

2 Ermita de las Nieves

Model boats, gifts from fishermen, adorn the interior of this culturally important small church. A Flemish triptych dedicated to the Virgen de las Nieves ("Virgin of the Snows") dominates.

3 Bajada de la Rama

This 4 August celebratio *(below)* has its origins in a Guanche rain-making ceremony. Revellers come as much for the street party as for the tradition of beating the ocean with pine branches

4 Beach

Of the two available beaches, most opt for the one that's further from the port (left). There's no golden sand, but the calm, clean waters make up for the pebbles.

5 Ferries to Tenerife

Boat trips to Tenerife leave from ıe port between 6:30am and :30pm and reach Santa Cruz, the ısland's capital, in just over an hour.

6 Seafood Restaurants

Sample the catch of the day in ne of many family-run restaurants n the seafront *(right)*. If you can't ecide on a dish, order a *parrillada* nixed grill) of fish and seafood.

7 Fishing

If eating other people's spoils isn't enough, join the locals on the wharf *(below)* and try to catch your own lunch. Better still, you could ask around to see if anyone has room on his boat for an extra fisherman. Or just sip a coffee and watch the local fishermen repairing their nets in the harbour.

8 Old Relics

Puerto de las Nieves ıeems to be a magnet or disused devices from ong-gone glory days. The odd-looking 19th-century vindmill in Avenida de los Poetas is the only one of its kind on the island, vhile the old jib crane and mekiln now serve to fill ourists' photo albums.

9 Reproduction of Maipés de Abajo

The Guanche burial site at this location was destroyed by construction work. Today, only a small reproduction of the tombs can be viewed here. In contrast, the Maipés de Arriba *(see p41)*, in the Agaete Valley, survived the development of that area.

10 Diving and Surfing

Those who find the pace of the village a little slow may like to try out local watersports *(right)*. Scuba diving is popular around he cliffs near Dedo de Dios, while surfers prefer Punta de las Viejas, just north of the port.

Highs and Lows

The natural harbour that is now Puerto de las Nieves played an important, if slightly disloyal, role during the final years of the Conquest. From here, the region's ruler was bundled onto a boat to be baptized on the mainland. The Spanish conquerors also launched their assault on Tenerife from this port. Later on, Puerto de las Nieves underwent periods of alternate ruin and prosperity, as trade with America ebbed and flowed.

Puerto de la Luz, c. 1895–1900

TOP 10 Moments in History

1 Volcanic Origins

Like all of the Canary Islands, Gran Canaria is volcanic in origin and first emerged from the ocean 15 million years ago. A second spurt of volcanic activity created the northeast of the island 11 million years later. Happily, the volcanoes have been extinct for 3,000 years.

2 Arrival of the First Inhabitants

Mystery shrouds the island's original inhabitants. Most historians argue that the Guanches arrived from North Africa around 2,000 BC. Others believe they were Vikings, or even Atlanteans! With the discovery of Cro-Magnon skulls, some have suggested that Cro-Magnon and Mediterranean man may have co-existed on the island.

Mummified Guanche from Gran Canaria

3 Early Exploration

Although the Portuguese and Mallorcans had both sailed past the island, it wasn't until 1405 that Jean de Bethencourt *(below)* landed. Though he had successfully taken Fuerteventura and Lanzarote, he could not overcome the tough Canarios. Juan Rejón had better luck in 1478, when he managed to set up the hamlet Real de Las Palmas the island's future capital.

4 Baptism and Defeat

The natives proved no match for the Spanish invaders. The northern chief, Tenesor Semidan, was captured, baptized, and enlisted in the Spanish cause. Final defeat came in 1483, when many of the remaining fighters jumped into a deep ravine rather than live in slavery.

Bethencourt landing on Gran Canaria

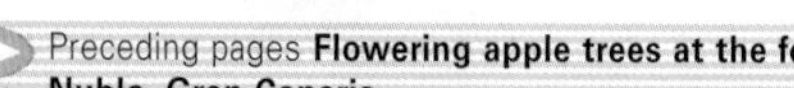

Preceding pages **Flowering apple trees at the foot of Roque Nublo, Gran Canaria**

5 Pirates Attack

The archipelago's strategic position on the major trade routes brought fortune, but also trouble in the form of pirates. The defensive wall surrounding Las Palmas did little to protect it when Sir Francis Drake attacked in 1595, though he failed to defeat the locals. A more successful 10-day assault by Dutch corsair Pieter Van Der Does devastated the capital in 1599, and scores of churches and other historical buildings were sacked and burnt.

Pieter Van der Does' assault on Gran Canaria

6 Mass Emigration

Following Columbus's discovery of the New World, thousands of islanders headed across the ocean, settling throughout the Americas from Texas to Argentina. Most, however, made for the Caribbean islands and Venezuela. To this day, Venezuela is known as the "eighth island" due to its strong family links with the archipelago.

7 Boom and Bust

Contact with Latin America led to fierce competition and Gran Canaria's sugar cane industry was ruined by tumbling prices. The wine and cochineal (food colouring) trades went the same way and, by the end of the 19th century, things were looking desperate, rekindling the mass exodus to Latin America.

8 Getting Connected

The development of Puerto de la Luz in 1881 was to change the island's fortunes forever. It soon became the archipelago's principal port and today it is one of Europe's largest. The Canary Islands' first airport was built just south of Las Palmas in 1930.

9 Franco Launches his Military Coup

When Spanish officials got wind of a rebellious general in March 1936, they quickly shipped him off to the Canary Islands. Their foresight didn't pay off and, in July of the same year, General Francisco Franco and his followers launched an uprising from their headquarters in Las Palmas. It was the beginning of the Spanish Civil War. In 1939, Franco came to power and decades of Fascist rule began in Spain, only ending with his death in 1975.

10 Tourism Takes Hold

After the failed industries of earlier centuries, the islands needed a new and more stable source of jobs and income. Salvation arrived in the 1960s in the form of mass construction, and tomato plantations were soon giving way to high-rise hotels. The tables had turned, and tourism is now the pillar of the archipelago's economy. Rather than somewhere to escape from, Gran Canaria has now become a favoured destination for immigrants.

Franco in Las Palmas, 1955

Guanches, the orginal inhabitants of the Canary Islands, were also known as Canarios.

Left **Museo Elder de la Ciencia y la Tecnología** Right **Museo Néstor**

Top 10 Museums

1 Casa de Colón, Las Palmas

Take a fascinating journey through the history of navigation and the discovery of America in one of the island's most attractive buildings *(see pp8–9)*.

Traditional pottery at the Museo Canario

2 Museo Canario, Las Palmas

A mesmerizing peek into the Canary Islands' enigmatic pre-Hispanic culture is provided here, with some superb exhibits that have been unearthed around the islands *(see pp12–13)*.

3 Museo Elder de la Ciencia y la Tecnología, Las Palmas

The capital's science museum offers a perfect blend of education and entertainment, with plenty of interactive exhibits to keep visitors of all ages amused *(see p66)*.

4 Museo Néstor, Las Palmas

Admire the finest works of Gran Canarian Modernist maestro, Néstor Martín Fernández de la Torre, in the Neo-Classical Pueblo Canario, designed and built in the 1930s by the artist's brother, Miguel. One of the museum's highlights, the eight-panel *Poema del Atlántico (Poem of the Atlantic)* is widely con-sidered to be the artist's finest work, though the sensitivity shown in *Poem of the Earth* is also remarkable *(see p66)*.

5 Museo de Historia de Agüimes

Inhabited since Guanche times, Agüimes has a full and interesting past that warrants a museum in its honour. Visitors can learn about the area's many ancient legends and superstitions, a product of its great ethnic mix. Displayed in a handsome 17th-century mansion, the exhibits are well laid out and information is provided in three languages. *C/ Juan Alvarado y Saz 42 • Map E4 • 928 78 54 53 • 9am–5pm Tue–Sun • Adm charge • No disabled access*

6 Casa Museo Antonio Padrón, Gáldar

Many of Antonio Padrón's colour-ful paintings portray Canarian customs and daily life, though the collection here does include a number of his Expressionist works. The museum is set in the artist's studio, a charming building in his home town *(see p75)*.

Casa Museo Antonio Padrón

7 Museo de los Patronos de la Virgen, Teror

The sponsors of Gran Canaria's most important statue of the Virgin resided for centuries in this sparkling example of Canarian architecture. Today it is preserved as a museum, complete with period furniture and paintings. There is also a patio and a small chapel *(see p20)*.

Interior of CAAM

8 CAAM, Las Palmas

Set in the historic quarter of Las Palmas is this ultra-modern art gallery. The building is brought to life by its varied temporary exhibitions by Spanish, African and Latin-American artists *(see p68)*.

9 Ecomuseo Casa-Alfar Panchito, La Atalaya

Visit the cave-home and workshop of a master of traditional pottery, and see a side of Canarian life that is all but lost. *Camino de la Picota 11 • Map E3 • 928 28 82 70 • 9.30am–1.30pm, 4–7.30pm Tue–Thu, 9am–1pm Fri–Sat • Adm charge*

10 Centro de Interpretación de Guayadeque

Cave living, past and present, gets its own museum in this spectacular ravine setting *(see pp28–9)*.

Top 10 Museum Exhibits

1 *Poema del Atlántico,* Museo Néstor
Néstor's magnum opus is an eight-panel work showing the ocean at different times of day.

2 Drawing Room, Museo de los Patronos de la Virgen
This room fronting the town square contains some fine antique furniture and portraits.

3 *Piedad,* Casa Museo Antonio Padrón
Antonio Padrón died before completing his final painting.

4 Foucault's Pendulum, Museo Elder de la Ciencia y la Tecnología
Patient folk can watch this massive pendulum gradually knocking over small posts, proving that the earth rotates.

5 Idolo de Tara, Museo Canario
The island's largest and most important pre-Hispanic idol.

6 *Poema de la Tierra,* Museo Néstor
This reflective work depicts the seasons and the times of day.

7 Astrolabe, Casa de Colón
This 15th-century navigational device is one of a kind.

8 Water Mill, Centro de Interpretación de Guayadeque
An interactive model explains the workings of a water mill.

9 Superstitions and Witchcraft, Museo de la Historia de Agüimes
Spinning panels relate the surprising beliefs of early settlers.

10 Workshop, Ecomuseo Casa-Alfar Panchito
Enter the primitive workshop of the ceramics maestro for an insight into Guanche pottery.

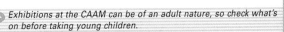

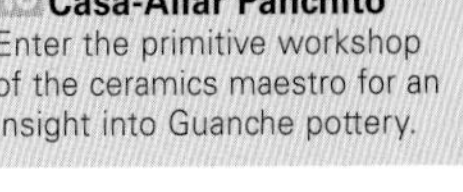

Exhibitions at the CAAM can be of an adult nature, so check what's on before taking young children.

Left **Templo Parroquial de San Sebastián** Right **Catedral de Santa Ana**

Top 10 Churches

1 Catedral de Santa Ana, Las Palmas

Extending across 7,000 sq m (75,000 sq ft), the capital's cathedral is an impressive blend of architectural styles. Some important Luján Pérez sculptures and remnants of the original Gothic structure can be seen inside *(see pp10–11)*.

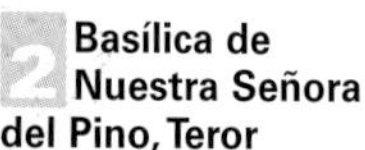

2 Basílica de Nuestra Señora del Pino, Teror

Rebuilt and renovated countless times, this immense basilica has drawn numerous pilgrims since the 16th century *(see pp22–23)*.

Basílica de Nuestra Señora del Pino

3 Templo Parroquial de San Sebastián, Agüimes

Follow the maze of cobbled alleys in Agüimes and eventually you'll reach the magnificent Templo Parroquial de San Sebastián. A supreme example of Canarian Neo-Classical architecture, it has the air of a cathedral rather than a church. Although started in 1796, the church was not completed until 1940. *Plaza Nuestra Señora del Rosario • Map E4*

4 Iglesia de Santiago de los Caballeros, Gáldar

The distinctive feature of this church is that it wasn't built to a typical Canarian design, but rather in a blend of Baroque and Neo-Classical styles. Check out the *pila verde* (green font), allegedly where the natives were baptized when the Spanish first took over. *Plaza de Santiago • Map C1*

5 Basílica de San Juan Bautista, Telde

The façade of Telde's main church is as forbidding as its heavy wooden door, evoking thoughts of medieval castles. Inside, a Flemish altarpiece, among the most precious works of art in the Canary Islands, outshines the main Baroque altarpiece. The figure of Christ was modelled from corn paste by Michoacan Mexicans in 1550 *(see p90)*.

Parroquia de San Juan Bautista

Most churches don't have set opening times, but it's better to visit in the morning.

6 Parroquia de Nuestra Señora de la Candelaria, Moya

This large 20th-century church, with twin bell towers and a flawless rose window, is the focal point of sleepy Moya, but its most memorable feature is its vertiginous location, perched precariously atop a rugged ravine *(see p76)*.

7 Iglesia de Nuestra Señora de la Concepción, Agaete

The bright red dome crowning Agaete's church sets it apart from other churches built in a similar Neo-Classical style.
C/Juan Valls y Roca 1 • Map C2

Iglesia de Santa Lucía

8 Iglesia de Santa Lucía

This pretty church of 1905 is likened to a mosque due to its pronounced dome. *Plaza de Santa Lucía, Santa Lucía de Tirajana • Map D4*

9 Parroquia de San Juan Bautista, Arucas

Behind the ornate façade of the island's most striking church, built largely from volcanic rock, lies an equally impressive interior full of sculptures, paintings, stained-glass windows and a grand altarpiece *(see p76)*.

10 Iglesia de la Candelaria, Ingenio

This 20th-century church features sculptures of San José and San Blás by Luján Pérez *(see p11)*.
C/Hermanos Fullana 5 • Map E4

Top 10 Ermitas

1 Ermita de la Virgen de la Cuevita, Artenara
The patron saint of cyclists resides in this small rock-face chapel *(see p82)*.

2 Ermita de las Nieves, Puerto de las Nieves
This small church started out as a shrine in a 15th-century fortified tower.

3 Ermita de San Antonio Abad, Las Palmas
Columbus is said to have prayed in this charming church before heading off to the New World.

4 Ermita de la Inmaculada Concepción, La Atalaya
This simple 18th-century church resembles a rural house.

5 Ermita de San Telmo, Las Palmas
This church was rebuilt in 1694 after the original 16th-century hermitage was destroyed by Dutch pirates.

6 Ermita de San Isidro, San Isidro (Teror)
Forebears of the current owners built this privately owned 17th-century church.

7 Ermita de San Sebastián, Agaete
This *mudéjar*-style hermitage has an elaborate ceiling.

8 Ermita de San Isidro El Viejo, Gáldar
This mosque-like building is perhaps the island's smallest place of worship.

9 Ermita de San Roque, Valsequillo
This 20th-century church, built in traditional style, is backed by an impressive palm grove.

10 Ermita de Ayacata, Ayacata
In February, this pretty church in the mountains is enveloped in almond blossom.

Ermitas *can usually be viewed only from outside, but you can contact the individual parishes if you're keen to see the interior.*

Left **Cueva Pintada** Right **Cuatro Puertas**

TOP 10 Guanche Sites

1 Cueva Pintada

In 1860, a local farmer stumbled across this painted cave, uncovering probably the most important archeological find – and certainly the finest set of aboriginal paintings – in the whole archipelago. In July 2006, after more than 20 years, the Cueva Pintada reopened to the public. Only a limited number of visitors are allowed in, so book tickets in advance *(see p75)*.

2 Tufia

This settlement is unusual as it has examples of both types of aboriginal home common to the island: cave dwellings, and the low stone houses unique to Gran Canaria. The coastal caves once inhabited by Guanches now house 21st-century troglodytes, but the stone constructions are still in their original state. Dominating the scene is an immense *tagoror*, where the elders would meet to make decisions *(see p87)*.

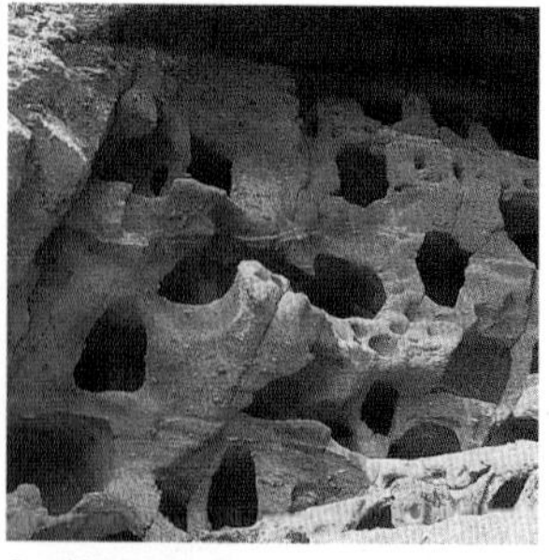

Cenobio de Valerón

3 Cuatro Puertas

If other aboriginal sites on the island didn't impress, visit Cuatro Puertas. This is the most remarkable man-made cave on Gran Canaria and therefore in the archipelago. The large room with four "doors" was once a sacred place. A clear path marks the route around the site *(see p88)*.

Túmulo de La Guancha

4 Túmulo de La Guancha

Though rather average when compared to the tombs of Egyptian royalty, this Guanche cemetery outshines others scattered around the island. It's thought that the central sepulchre contained the *guanarteme* (king), while the aristocracy were laid to rest around him *(see p78)*.

5 Cenobio de Valerón

Built without the use of modern tools, this cluster of miniature artificial caves represents an awe-inspiring feat of early engineering. For years, experts believed it to be a convent, but it is now widely agreed that the caves were used to store grain *(see p74)*.

Some sites are open to the public, but others require special permission from the cabildo *(council). Tel: 928 219 421 ext 4441.*

6 Maipés de Arriba

Featuring around 500 tombs, the Maipés de Arriba may have been the principal burial ground for lowly Guanches. Look out for the different styles of tomb, particularly the circular towers, which were almost certainly the last resting-place of aboriginal aristocracy. A similar site closer to the coast, the Maipés de Abajo, was destroyed by modern development; there's a small-scale reproduction of it in Puerto de las Nieves *(see p31)*. *Map C2*

7 Letreros de Balos

Cave drawings have been found across the islands, but the sheer variety at this site in the Balos ravine is remarkable. Some of the etchings seem to depict fertility symbols, a common theme in pre-Hispanic Canarian culture. There are even some alphabetical inscriptions, linked to the North African Libic-Berber peoples *(see p90)*.

8 Arteara

The island's most important burial site boasts an impressive location, nestled in a palm grove in the Fataga ravine. Information panels explain the piles of rocks before you, and there's also a small information centre. *Map D5 • Information centre: 928 77 15 50 (ring in advance to arrange guided tour). Open 10am–4pm Mon–Fri*

9 La Fortaleza de Ansite

The Guanches' last stronghold is pock-marked with caves overlooking the Tirajana ravine. You can imagine the islanders' plight as they tried in vain to repel the Spaniards, then threw themselves into the void shouting the patriotic motto *"Atis Tirma"*. *Map D4*

Roque Bentayga

10 Roque Bentayga

Numerous dwellings and grain stores have been unearthed around this huge monolith, which was considered sacred by the Guanches *(see pp24, 81)*.

None of these sites has disabled access.

Left **Montañón Negro** Right **Dunas de Maspalomas**

TOP 10 Beauty Spots

1 Montañón Negro

Canarian pine stands out against the stark black landscape of Gran Canaria's most recent, yet long extinct, volcano. Its last eruption some 3,000 years ago left a deep and arresting crater, the Caldera de los Pinos de Gáldar. *Map C3*

2 Pilancones

Though not as lush or as dense as its northern counterpart, Tamadaba, Pilancones is still impressive. Almost 5,800 ha (14,332 acres) of Canarian pine forest, it's an unrivalled place for bird-watching. Look out for the great spotted woodpecker *(see p95)*.

3 Los Tilos de Moya

Outside of the Botanical Garden, this is Gran Canaria's only area of *laurisilva (see pp14–15)*. Stroll through this lost world of vegetation, of a kind almost wiped out in Europe in the last Ice Age. Myrtle, willow and heather flourish alongside the many laurel species *(see p75)*.

Presa de las Niñas

4 Barranco de los Cernícalos

This remarkable ravine boasts year-round running water, a rarity on Gran Canaria. Admire the changing vegetation as you reach the highest waterfall, an easy walk that takes you through willow trees and olive groves. You might also spot some rare plants unique to the island. Look out for the Canarian bellflower and Tenteniguada viper's bugloss *(see p16)*. Access to the ravine is via Lomo Magullo. *Map E3*

Barranco de Guayadeque

5 Barranco de Guayadeque

Fascinating flora, important heritage and an unusual way of life coexist in the most spectacular of Gran Canaria's ravines *(see pp28–9)*.

6 Jardín Botánico Viera y Clavijo

Enjoy the riches of Canarian flora in this perfectly laid-out garden, an easy day trip from the capital, Las Palmas. As well as native plants, there's a variety of tropical and imported species that thrive in the island's mild climate *(see pp14–15)*.

7 Presa de las Niñas

The island's most attractive reservoir is also its most popular, and on weekends you will have to share its beauty with more than a few picnickers. In the week, you can enjoy a peaceful stroll in the small pine wood and imagine perhaps that you are in Canada rather than the Canaries. There is also a well-equipped picnic area and campsite here, though you will need a permit from the *cabildo* (council) to make use of the latter. *(see p96)*.

Pinar de Tamadaba

8 Pinar de Tamadaba

Enjoy the view from this peaceful spot, rich in Canarian pine and home to some incredibly rare endemic flowers, found only in this corner of the island. In the Guanche language, Tamadaba meant "hollow", though much of the forest is in fact higher than the surrounding land *(see p81)*.

9 Los Azulejos

As you reach Mogán from La Aldea de San Nicolás, the sparse cliffs suddenly light up with a rainbow of colours, ranging from blue to brown and passing through every shade of green and yellow. In winter, small waterfalls trickle down the cliffs, further enhancing their beauty. *Map B4*

10 Dunas de Maspalomas

There's nowhere else quite like these magnificent golden dunes, nestled in the heart of the tourist resort. If you're feeling energetic, take the tough trek through the shifting dunes to the point where the hotels eventually peter out and nothing but sand can be seen *(see pp18–19)*.

Top 10 Local Fauna

1 Gran Canaria Giant Lizard *(Gallotia stehlini)*
Up to 80 cm (30 inches) long, it's often visible on warm rocks.

2 Gran Canaria Skink *(Chalcides sexlineatus)*
These small lizards scurry off when humans approach.

3 Blue Chaffinch *(Fringilla teydea polatzeki)*
Spot one in the pine forest north of Mogán, if you're lucky.

4 Great Spotted Woodpecker *(Dendrocopos major)*
Black and white, with a flash of orange feathers. Endangered, but seen in the pine forests.

5 Berthelot's Pipit *(Anthus berthelotii Bolle)*
Another, more common, fan of the island's pine forests.

6 Common Kestrel *(Falco tinnunculus Linnaeus)*
Abundant, but still impressive; look out for its mottled wings.

7 Barbary Falcon *(Falco pelegrinoides Temminck)*
Difficult to spot, especially as it has no preferred habitat.

8 Red-legged Partridge *(Alectoris rufa)*
Widespread across Gran Canaria, but rarely seen on neighbouring islands.

9 Stone Curlew *(Burhinus oedicnemus)*
The stone curlew has its home in the northern ravines, where its habitat is now under threat.

10 Lesser Short-toed Lark *(Callendrella rufescens)*
Its tawny crown appears in arid zones from Telde to Mogán.

In Mogán you can buy ceramics inspired by the multicoloured cliffs of Los Azulejos.

Left **Aguadulce** Right **Las Burras**

Top 10 Beaches

1 Maspalomas

This is an unrivalled place to sunbathe, bordered by the dazzling dunes *(see pp18–19)*.

Maspalomas

2 Las Canteras

Don your snorkel and swim with the fish in the crystalline waters of the capital's 2.8-km (1.7–mile) golden beach. A rocky reef (known as *La Barra*, "The Bar") keeps the waves back, making this a superb place for families to swim. Further south, the reef ends and surfers take advantage of the breaks. If you prefer to stay dry, take a gentle stroll along the promenade, stopping in La Puntilla for a seafood lunch. *Map N2*

Las Canteras

3 Amadores

Located in the sunniest part of the island, Amadores offers a wide crescent of golden sand with plentiful services and facilities such as windsurfing, diving and boat excursions as well as mini golf and golf courses nearby. The beach is also lined with restaurants and bars. The fabulous cliff walk between Amadores and nearby Puerto Rico gives superb views of the beach. *Map B5*

4 San Agustín

Most of the bathers here are Canarian daytrippers from the capital, but some tourists are getting wise to this gem. Calm waters border the black sand beach, split into three sections by rocky outcrops. *Map F4*

5 Montaña Arena

Untouched by the swathe of development that plagues the south coast, this stretch of dark sand has no amenities. Favoured by nudists, it is away from the crowds without being too far from civilization. To get there, park at the camp site west of Pasito Blanco, head for the stony beach and take a vertiginous path to the left. *Map C6*

6 Veneguera

This is another pristine beach favoured by nudists but largely ignored. After Veneguera village the roads are only passable by 4WD; otherwise, park and walk the last section. Backed by towering cliffs, the black sand and pebbles are lapped by a calm stretch of ocean. *Map B5*

Be wary of swimming on deserted beaches, where currents can be perilous, especially on the west and north coasts.

Broad expanse of golden sand at El Inglés

7 El Inglés

Maspalomas's closest neighbour is one of the island's busiest beaches, but it's large enough for all to enjoy its fine golden sand. For those who like a few amenities while they bathe, there's no lack of bars or sun-loungers and, as you'd expect, the resort here is well-served with restaurants and hotels *(see pp99,113,115)*. *Map D6*

8 El Juncal

Few sun-seekers venture to this secluded cove, but those who do are rewarded with exceptionally calm waters surrounded by stunning cliffs. From the GC2 heading west, take the exit after km 29, then keep heading left through the tomato plantations. Once you reach a plain, park and walk the last 20 minutes. *Map B2*

9 Aguadulce

Below the Guanche settlement of Tufia lies a quiet, sheltered cove with 140 m (459 ft) of golden sand, and good snorkelling and diving opportunities. Though easy to reach, this east-coast beach is often deserted, as the majority of holidaymakers prefer the guaranteed good weather further south. Watch the planes take off and land at the nearby airport, or contemplate the aboriginal ruins at Tufia *(see p87)*. *Map F3*

10 Las Burras

For those who don't mind a bit of wind, Las Burras is an alternative to the busier resort beaches further along the coast. A favourite with locals, the calm waters are perfect for those with children. *Map D6*

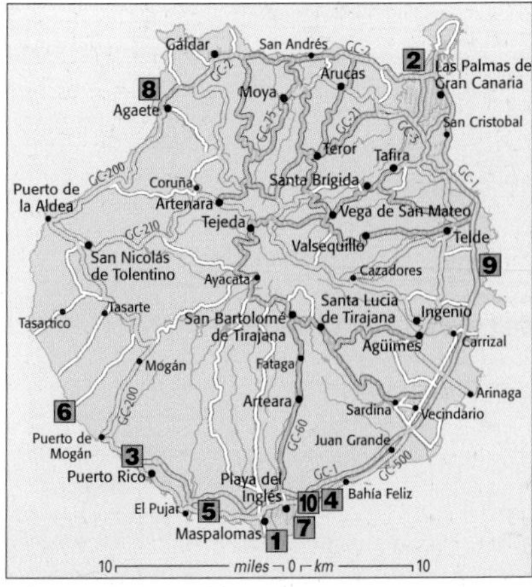

On busier beaches, respect the safety flags and listen for warnings on the loudspeakers.

Camel riding in Maspalomas

TOP 10 Outdoor Activities

1 Hiking

The possibilities are endless, ranging from short and easy hikes to the more challenging routes of the *caminos reales* ("royal ways") that were once the only way to negotiate the island. Always check locally to ensure that routes are safe or, better still, join an organized group. *Nortetrek: 636 578 586 • www.nortetrekgrancanaria.com • Rambling Roger: www.ramblingroger.com*

Real Club de Golf de Las Palmas

2 Golf

Golfers are well catered for on the island, with six 18-hole courses, plus a few nine-hole pitch and putts. The mild climate has made the sport a major draw. Most courses are in the south, although the prestigious Real Club de Golf *(see p27)* is just outside Las Palmas and the Las Palmeras Golf Sport Urban Resort is in Las Palmas itself. *Las Palmeras Golf Sport Urban Resort: Avda Dr Alfonso Chiscano Díaz s/n. 928 222 333. www.laspalmerasgolf.es*

3 Climbing

The volcanic terrain is a dream for climbers, in particular the central peaks. Roque Nublo alone boasts 12 routes, while Ayacata is another top spot more suited to beginners. *Map C3 • Canary Climbing Delegation: 928 290 652*

4 Parapente

You don't need to be super-fit to practise this adrenaline sport, but you do need a head for heights. Beginners can try a tandem jump. *928 157 000 • www.parapentelaspalmas.com*

5 Skydiving

For an alternative view of the Maspalomas dunes, try jumping out of a plane 3,500 m (11,480 ft) above the resort – strapped to an instructor, of course. *928 157 325 • www.skydivegrancanaria.es*

6 Helicopter Rides

You can book a 10–60-minute helicopter flight for a unique view of the Gran Canarian landscape. See the craggy west, the lush north, or the southern resorts. *Islas Helicopters: 928 157 965 • www.islas-helicopters.com*

Helicopter rides

7 Camel Riding

Explore the scenic Fataga ravine or the Maspalomas sand dunes on the back of a camel. *Map D4 (Fataga), D6 (Maspalomas) • 928 798 680*

Carry plenty of water when hiking or biking – the heat can be punishing.

8 Cycling

Hardcore cyclists lap up the challenge posed by the island's mountain roads. Favourite routes are the Barranco de Arguineguin, Agüimes to Santa Lucía de Tirajana, and a tough circuit through Puerto de Mogán, Veneguera and Mogán. The less committed head for the high peaks by bus and freewheel back. Join an organized group tour or just hire your own bike. ✆ *928 766 832 • www.happy-biking.com*

Cycling in the south of the island

9 Canyoning

If you want to get to know parts of the island untouched by most visitors, take an excursion that includes hiking through dense vegetation and lowering yourself into rocky clefts. The varied terrain of the island makes it an ideal place for both novices and experienced canyoners. ✆ *928 766 168 • www.canariaventura.com*

10 Football

Most Spaniards love the "beautiful game", and Canarians are no exception. Even if you're not a habitual football fan, watching a match can be a wonderful way to spend a Sunday afternoon. Gran Canaria's biggest team, UD Las Palmas, has suffered a run of bad luck in recent years, but loyal fans still turn up at the impressive stadium to cheer on "the Yellows".
✆ *Estadio de Gran Canaria, c/ Fondos de Segura s/n, Las Palmas • Map E2 • 928 41 69 45 • www.udlaspalmas.es*

Top 10 Canarian Sports Stars

1 Juan Carlos Valerón
The talented *Primera Liga* midfielder has won more than 40 international caps.

2 Luis Doreste
With two Olympic gold medals, Doreste is among Spain's top sailing stars. Younger brother of José Luis *(see below)*.

3 Domingo Manrique
This four-time Olympian won gold at Barcelona in 1992 with his team mate Doreste.

4 Adelina Taylor
Taylor was crowned 2001 Spanish and European surfing champion.

5 Magüi Serna
At her peak in the 1990s, she was ranked in the world's top 20 female tennis players.

6 El Pollito de la Frontera
The "Little Chicken" was one of the big names in *Lucha Canaria* (team wrestling in a sand circle) since his mid-1990s debut.

7 Hermanas Ruano
Twin sisters Iballa and Daida regularly rank first and second in international windsurfing competitions.

8 Björn Dunkerbeck
Although Danish, this windsurfing star has long lived on the island, and he was world champion from 1988 through to 1999.

9 José Luis Doreste
Doreste competed in every Olympiad from Montreal (1976) to Atlanta (1996), winning gold at Seoul in 1988.

10 Antonio Alfonso (Tonono)
Finishing his football career at UD Las Palmas, he played in the national team 22 times.

Left **Surfing** Right **Diving**

TOP 10 Marine Activities

1 Surfing

Few European destinations offer such good surf, a fact made clear by the number of blond-streaked enthusiasts in search of the perfect wave. Schools operate in the south of the island, while the rougher northern coast has more appeal for experts. *PR Surfing: 628 10 40 25. www.prsurfing.com*

2 Diving

Whether your interest is marine life or sunken ships, diving in the seas off Gran Canaria is a satisfying affair. Marine species from Europe, Africa and even the Caribbean mingle here, and the high number of shipwrecks adds extra interest. Playa del Cabrón, Pasito Blanco and Sardina del Norte all offer superlative dives, while the bulk of the wrecks are off the coast of Las Palmas. *Sunsub: 928 77 81 65. www.sunsub.com • 7 Mares Las Canteras: 928 46 00 35. www.7mares.es*

3 Windsurfing

Professionals can't get enough of Pozo Izquierdo, host to an international competition in the summer, though its waters are not suited for novices. The school here takes those starting out in the sport to calmer seas until they are up to windsurfing with the experts. *Centro Internacional de Windsurfing: 928 12 14 00. www.pozo-ciw.com*

Windsurfing

Yachts moored in Puerto de Mogán harbour

4 Sailing

Whether you want to hire a boat and go it alone, or learn how to sail, Gran Canaria offers plenty of possibilities. The season is from April to October, though enthusiasts can be catered for all year round. *Puerto Rico Sailing School: 928 56 07 62*

5 Thalassotherapy

This soothing treatment massages away aches with jets of heated seawater. There are centres in Las Palmas, Maspalomas, Agaete and Amadores.

6 Snorkelling

Gran Canaria is a superb snorkelling destination. There's no need to stray further than the capital's beach, Las Canteras, for encounters with parrotfish, octopus, wrasse and countless species of bream.

7 Swimming

Canarian waters are blessed ith a lack of anything that bites. n the other hand, do not expect arm seas, as this is the Atlantic. ne south and east coasts are enerally safe, though currents nd strong waves plague the orth and west. If you fancy a p in the north, head for one of e natural pools *(see page 77)*.

8 Fishing

Whether it's side by side with e locals on the wharf, or out at ea, there is fishing aplenty. The est deep-sea trips are out of uerto Rico, where tuna, marlin nd swordfish abound in summer. *Dorado: 928 569 306. ww.marlincanariasportfishing.com*

hing, Puerto de las Nieves

9 Boat Trips

Charter a luxury yacht, gaze own into the ocean from a ass-bottomed boat, or live it up a booze cruise. Puerto Rico is e best place from which to set il, but there are also trips from s Palmas and Playa del Inglés.

10 Kayaking

There is no better way to ppreciate the island's diverse astline than from a kayak. eginners can get started at Playa e las Canteras, while the more venturous may like to join a tour the southern coast, stopping off normally inaccessible beaches. *Canariaventura: 928 76 61 68. ww.canariaventura.com*

Top 10 Underwater Encounters

1 Parrotfish
Whether you're snorkel-ling or on a deep dive, you are almost guaranteed to see the island's most emblematic underwater creature.

2 Bluefin Damselfish
These fish are abundant, but you won't tire of seeing the vivid blue glint contrasted against the black scales.

3 Angel Shark
The most commonly sighted shark, often mistaken for a ray due to its flat body.

4 Ornate Wrasse
The blue-green shimmer of this fish is a familiar but pleasing sight on any dive.

5 Octopus
Frequently lurks on the seabed, but seen from surface level down to 100 m (330 ft).

6 Spiny Butterfly Ray
This mottled fish, which measures up to 1.5 m (5 ft), hides, unnoticed, in the sand.

7 Tiger Moray
One of a number of serpentine fish, the Tiger Moray is unmistakable, with its bright yellow skin and evil-looking teeth.

8 Trumpetfish
A comical species that can change colour according to its mood. Frequent on deeper dives.

9 Scorpionfish
Numerous species of this spiky fish swim in the Canarian seas, usually favouring rocky areas.

10 Shipwrecks
Ships have been sinking off these shores ever since ports were built, so there are wrecks aplenty sprinkled around the coast.

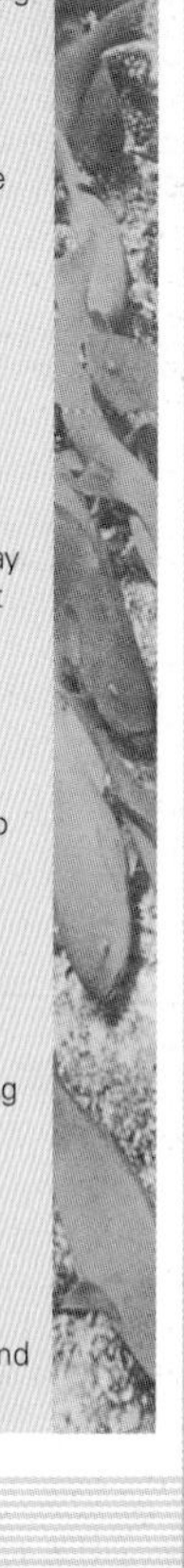

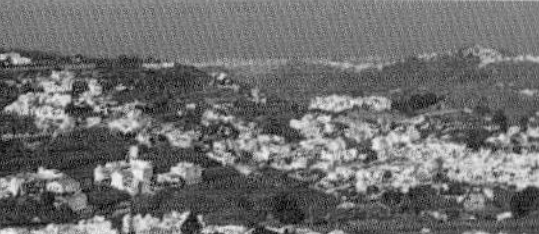

Left **Tamadaba drive** Right **View from Balcón de Zamora (Teror to Artenara)**

TOP 10 Hikes and Drives

Village of Fataga (Agüimes to Maspalomas)

1 Agüimes to Maspalomas via Temisas, Santa Lucía de Tirajana and Fataga (drive)

Break up this winding drive with stops at quaint *pueblos* Temisas *(see p89)* and Fataga, and at the *mirador* (viewpoint) on the road to Maspalomas. A detour takes you to the La Sorrueda reservoir and on to the Fortaleza de Ansite, south of Santa Lucía de Tirajana. *Map E4–D6*

2 Barranco de los Cernícalos (hike)

Take the road out of Lomo Magullo towards Los Arenales. A clear path leads you along the lush ravine, where a stream trickles throughout the year. As well as appealing to lovers of flora, the hike rewards all with its impressive finale: a series of ever-higher waterfalls. Allow about three hours for this out-and-back walk. *Map E3*

3 Tamadaba (drive)

The fantastic views and lus scenery make this short circula drive a favourite. Follow the GC216 from Cruz de Acusa, nea Artenara, and take the loop arour Gran Canaria's finest pine fores The road is one-way. *Map C3*

4 The West Coast (drive)

Not for the faint-hearted, the road from Agaete to Mogán has stunning coastal views. Stop off Playa de la Aldea for a seafood lunch before turning inland. The Moorish village of Veneguera warrants a stop. Look out too for the colourful cliffs of Los Azulejo *(see p43)*. *Map C2–B4*

5 Teror to Artenara (drive)

The highlights of this drive along the GC21 are the stretch overlooking the Barranco de Valsendero and two superlative *miradors*, Balcón de Zamora and Los Pinos de Gáldar. *Map D2–C*

6 Santa Lucía de Tirajana to Fortaleza de Ansite (hike)

This three-hour hike leads you through idyllic countryside to th

West Coast drive

ortaleza de Ansite *(see p96)*. ake the path leading from km 49 f the GC65, then keep left at all orks. While here, visit the dazzling a Sorrueda reservoir. ✎ *Map D4*

7 Gáldar to Moya via Fontanales (drive)

he GC220 passes Hoya de 'ineda, a troglodyte village, efore reaching the Pinos de iáldar pine forest. Pause at the uperb Mirador de Los Pinos de iáldar before taking the GC70 ast Fontanales and then a pec-tacular side road, the ;C700, on to Moya. ✎ *Map C1–D2*

8 Barranco de la Virgen (hike)

Starting from Valleseco, this ree-hour hike takes you through alsendero before descending to the Barranco de la Virgen nd on to Las Madres. As the egetation changes om pine to aurel, keep an ye out for rare ative flora such s houseleeks. Overhead, kestrels, lackcaps and blue ts vie for space.) *Map D2*

9 The Dam Circuit (hike)

This breathtaking hike skirts ree of the island's reservoirs. tarting from the GC605 north of resa de las Niñas, it hugs the oria dam and passes north of hira. The walk takes seven ours and ends at Cruz Grande, ut you could break for the night t Los Cercados. ✎ *Map C4–D4*

0 Mogán to Pico de las Nieves (drive)

fter heavy rain, waterfalls start) appear along the winding road at leads to the island's highest oint *(see p25)*. ✎ *Map B4–D3*

Top 10 Miradors

1 Pico de Bandama

Few viewpoints offer such variety; from the crater's peak, you can see capital, coast and mountains *(see p26)*.

2 Pico de las Nieves

Lucky folk see the coast from the island's highest point; many get only mist *(see p25)*.

3 Degollada de Becerra

On a clear day, Mt Teide makes a fine backdrop to this already stunning view of Roque Bentayga, Tejeda and the Acusa flatlands.

4 Roque Nublo

Hiking to Gran Canaria's most famous monolith gives a unique view of the island's centre – the only one without the rock itself *(see p24)*.

5 Mirador del Balcón, La Aldea de San Nicolás

After driving the white-knuckle west coast, catch your breath contemplating the sheer cliffs.

6 Tamadaba

Pico de Tamadaba is a half-hour walk from the Casa Forestal in Pinar de Tamadaba *(see p43)*. Look over the pine forest, Artenara, Tenerife and sometimes even La Gomera.

7 Barranco de Fataga

A well-equipped *mirador*, with a restaurant and a superb view over the Fataga ravine.

8 Cima Pedro González

The Ayagaures dam, with its pretty rural village, is visible at the end of the ravine.

9 Cruz Grande

Central viewpoint over the Barranco de las Tederas and Pilancones forest *(see p42)*.

10 Los Pinos de Gáldar

Look into the depths of the imposing crater, dotted with Canarian pine trees.

If you're driving, you'll find that petrol stations are not in abundance, so fill up whenever you get the chance.

Left **Palmitos Park** Right **Aqualand Maspalomas water park**

Top 10 Children's Days Out

1 Palmitos Park

The Chamoriscan ravine provides a marvellous setting for this tropical paradise, home to primates, reptiles and countless exotic birds. Regular shows feature bike-riding parrots and enormous birds of prey. Calmer options include the aquarium, butterfly house and a large walk-through birdcage. Don't miss the mini-farm where children can pet very well cared-for animals *(see p95)*.

2 Sioux City, San Agustín

Spend a day in the Wild West and experience daring bank hold-ups, stampeding cattle and sudden shoot-outs. Friday night is barbecue night, when parents can enjoy the saloon and dancing girls, while the children are treated to a lasso show. *Cañon del Aguila • Map D6 • 928 762 573 • 10am–5pm Tue–Sun (and 8pm–midnight Fri) • Adm charge • www.siouxcity.es*

Sioux City

3 Museo Elder de la Ciencia y la Tecnología, Las Palmas

When you first arrive and see the mottos "Forbidden not to touch" and "Museum is not mausoleum", you know that the kids are going to enjoy themselves. Favourites include the flight simulator, TV studio and Imax cinema. There is also a science-themed play area for the smallest visitors, aged 3–6 years *(see pp36, 66)*.

4 Water Parks

There are 33 slides at Aqualand Maspalomas, the largest wate park on the island. There are also smaller parks closer to the resorts of Puerto Rico and Maspalomas *Aqualand Maspalomas: Ctra Palmitos Park, km 3. Map C5. 928 14 05 25. www.aqualand.es/maspalomas. 10am–5pm daily, (Jul-Aug 10am–6pm). Adm charge*

5 Yellow Submarine, Puerto de Mogán

Descend 25 m (82 ft) below the surface of the waves on 45-minute journey that take in a shipwreck and diverse marine life. *Map B5 • 928 5 51 08 • Boats leave hourly 10am–5pm daily • Adm charge • No disabled access • www.atlantida-submarine.com*

6 Horse Riding

A mountain or coastal ride i a lovely way to see the island's countryside. There are centres ir San Mateo and Maspalomas. *Happy Horse • 658 92 52 86*

Yellow Submarine

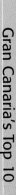

7 **Cocodrilo Park, Corralillos**
Europe's largest crocodile anctuary is also a haven for ther mistreated animals. There re over 300 crocodiles, tropical nd Canarian fish, other reptiles, arantulas, a parrot show and a amily of tigers. *GC104, Ctra Los Coralillos, km 5 • Map E4 • 928 78 47 25 10am–5pm Sun–Fri (parrot show: noon; rocodile feeding: 1pm) • Adm charge*

8 **Whales and Dolphins, Puerto Rico**
Get up close and personal with vhales and dolphins. Boat excursions depart from Puerto Rico harbour and include a useful commentary on these amazing animals *Puerto Base • Map B5 • 928 56 22 29 • www.dolphin-whale.com*

Holiday World

9 **Holiday World, Maspalomas**
There are carousels, bumper cars and a roller coaster for kids, bars and a disco for grown ups. *Avda Touroperador Tui • Map D6 • 928 73 04 98 • 6pm–midnight daily (summer), 5–11pm Sun–Thu, 5pm–midnight Fri–Sat (winter) • Adm charge*

10 **Go-karting**
Family fun with everything from mini cars and bikes for under-fives, and pint-sized motorbikes and full-size go-karts that reach 80 kmh (50 mph). *Gran Karting Club: Ctra General del Sur, km 46 • Map E5 • 928 15 71 90 • http://grancanaria.grankarting.com • 11am–10pm daily (summer), 11am–9pm daily (winter) • Adm charge*

Top 10 Tips for Families

1 **Sun**
Use a high factor sunblock and keep kids inside in the middle of the day.

2 **Sightseeing**
Under-12s often get half-price entry, and under-fives go free. Ask about family tickets.

3 **Beaches**
For a safer swim, head for the calm waters off Las Canteras and Arguineguin.

4 **Noise**
Canarians are incredibly tolerant of noise, so don't worry about your kids getting rowdy – except in churches.

5 **Car Hire**
If you need a child or baby seat, book in advance, as smaller companies may have limited numbers available.

6 **Escape the Resorts**
As an alternative to resort attractions, consider horse riding in the mountains, or visiting the capital's parks.

7 **Boat Trips**
The best options are glass-bottomed vessels or those that offer watersports.

8 **Accommodation**
An extra bed for a child under 12 is usually half-price. Younger children often go free and a cot is usually gratis.

9 **Restaurants**
Canarians love kids, although upmarket places may be wary of accepting them, especially in the evening. Children's portions are rarely available.

10 **Quiet Towns**
Small town centres like Teror, Firgas and Agüimes are virtually traffic-free, so you can feel safer about your children wandering around.

Left **Cabalgata de los Reyes Magos** Right **Fiesta de Nuestra Señora del Pino**

TOP 10 Traditional Fiestas

1 Cabalgata de los Reyes Magos (Procession of the Three Kings)

Melchior, Balthazar and Casper ride through the capital's streets on camels, throwing sweets to kids, who later get presents from the kings. Shops open until 2am for late-night gift-buying, and there are parties in the streets and makeshift bars of Triana. *5 Jan, Las Palmas*

2 Carnaval

Don your best costume and get ready for two months of *murgas* (satirical singing), *comparsas* (dancing competitions) and the all-important crowning of the drag queen. The party culminates with the burial of the sardine, a bizarre spectacle with mock mourners weeping because their fun has ended for another year. The most extravagant parties are in Las Palmas and Maspalomas. *Feb–Mar, island-wide*

Carnaval

3 Semana Santa (Holy Week)

This is a sombre affair, featuring solemn processions silencing towns across the island. On Good Friday, Las Palmas women don traditional dress and carry a sculpture of Christ along red carpets in Vegueta. There are similar processions island-wide on Easter Sunday, though none are quite as emotionally charged as their counterparts in mainland Spain. *Mar–Apr, island-wide*

4 Día de Canarias (Canary Islands Day)

Although relatively new, this commemoration of Canarian autonomy celebrates all that is time-honoured in the islands. Traditional costume is obligatory as merrymakers play the *timple* (a small guitar) and dance as their ancestors did. Local food and drink are dished out freely, so this is a great time for a visit. *30 May, island-wide*

5 Fiesta de San Juan

Revellers leap bonfires and toss oranges into the ocean against a backdrop of fireworks. Celebrated with gusto on Playa de las Canteras, as well as in Arucas and Telde, the festival coincides with the founding of Las Palmas, so the party in the capital is particularly impressive. *23–24 Jun, Las Palmas and other places*

Festival de San Juan

6 Corpus Christi

The tradition of flower-petal arpets has been lost in many arts of Spain, but is still firmly a art of Canarian culture. Don't iss the mammoth carpet laid ut before Las Palmas cathedral; 's always a true work of art. *un, Las Palmas and other towns*

7 Bajada de la Rama (Taking Down of the Branches)

his is a colourful pre-Hispanic ain-making ritual in which locals rocess to the ocean and beat it vith pine branches. *4–5 Aug, gaete and Puerto de las Nieves*

ajada de la Rama

8 Fiesta de Nuestra Señora del Pino (Festival of Our ady of the Pine)

Pretty Teror is the setting for this uge party honouring the Canary slands' patron saint *(see pp22–3)*. *8 Sep, Teror*

9 Fiestas del Charco

This Guanche festival sees articipants wade through the nurky waters of the *charco* oond) to catch fish with their are hands. Strangely good fun. *11 Sep, Puerto de la Aldea*

10 Romerías

It feels like there is always a iesta somewhere in Gran Canaria. Each town or village hosts its own *romería* (pilgrimage), which s really a street party featuring raditional dancing and Canarian ood. *Year-round, island-wide*

Top 10 Contemporary Festivals

1 Opera Festival, Las Palmas

The Alfredo Kraus Auditorium hosts a series of operas. *Mar–Jun*

2 Film Festival, Las Palmas

Week-long festival of independent and mainstream films across the capital. *Mar*

3 Masdanza, Maspalomas

Contemporary dance festival with shows and workshops. *Oct*

4 Fiesta del Queso, Guía

Taste local cheese and sample Canarian culture. *April/May*

5 Gay Pride, Maspalomas

Exhibitions, fundraisers and a big street parade to promote equal rights. *May*

6 Feria del Caballo, Valsequillo

This horse festival is the most important agricultural celebration on the island. *May*

7 International Folklore Festival, Ingenio

Global music and dance celebrating Ingenio's multicultural citizens. *July*

8 Jazz & Más, Las Palmas

The capital becomes a stage for international jazz, mostly open-air. *July*

9 Traída del Agua, Lomo Magullo

A huge water-fight whose origins go back centuries. *First half of Aug*

10 Traída del Barro

Partygoers make hay in clay, at La Atalaya, the pottery capital of the island. *July*

Left **Santa Brígida market** Right **El Muelle seaside mall, Las Palmas**

10 Places to Shop

1 Mercadillo de San Mateo

The island's best farmers' market offers excellent local produce and local handicrafts, such as wicker and leather goods. Try the marinated olives and *pan de millo* (sweet yellow cornbread). *Behind bus station • Map D3 • 8am–8pm Sat, 8am–3pm Sun*

2 Mercadillo de Santa Brígida

Stock up your picnic hamper at this farmers' market. Along with locally-grown fruit and vegetables, there are first-rate cheeses and fresh bread. Get a handmade wooden toy for the little ones and a well-crafted walking stick to help you hike in the hills. *Under Municipal Park • Map E3 • 8am–8pm Sat, 8am–2pm Sun*

3 Mercado de Teror

Religious artifacts are the focus of Teror's market, though biscuits, cakes and olives also make an appearance. More modern stallholders have started selling items such as clothes, toys and cheap electrical goods too. *Plaza del Pino • Map D2 • 8am–2pm Sunday*

Tienda Artesania Canaria Las Palmitas

Vegueta Sunday market

4 Vegueta Sunday Market

Artisans gather in the streets behind the cathedral to sell ceramics, clothing, food and handicrafts, all of the finest quality. Stop for refreshments in one of the makeshift bars set up for the occasion and watch the folk-dancing display. *Plaza del Pilar • Map M5 • 10am–3pm Sun*

5 Museo de Piedras y Artesanía, Ingenio

This is the best place on the island to buy crafts and to watch artisans at work. The local speciality, embroidery, is on sale alongside tablecloths, serviettes, blankets and craftwork from other islands. *Camino Real de Gando 1 • Map E4 • 8am–6:30pm Mon–Sat, 8am–noon, Sun*

6 Seaside Malls, Las Palmas

El Muelle and Las Arenas are both well-equipped with chain stores and places to eat. The shops in El Muelle are more expensive than those in Las Arenas, but the former has a greater choice of cafés and restaurants, as well as cinemas and discos for the post-shopping experience *(see p69)*.

Don't forget to take some photo ID with you if you intend to pay by credit card.

7 Tienda Artesania Canaria Las Palmitas, Vegueta

Pick up ceramics and other locally-made *objets d'art* from this curiosity shop in the heart of the old quarter *(see p69)*.

8 Calle Mayor de Triana, Las Palmas de Gran Canaria

The Modernist buildings that line the city's most elite shopping street now house chain stores, such as Benetton and Marks and Spencer, but it's still a great place to wile away an afternoon. For unique purchases, head to the boutiques in the cobbled side streets, where you'll find one-off clothes shops, original handicrafts and specialist bookshops. ✎ *Map L4*

Calle Mayor de Triana

9 Vecindario

The island's third largest town is no beauty, but it has two large malls, and a high street stretching 3 km (2 miles). Visit the big chain stores, or the craft shop in Parque de la Era de Verdugo. ✎ *Map E5*

10 El Molino, Las Rosas

Visit the small chapel before stocking up on local foodstuffs, basketry and hand-rolled cigars. The embroidered tablecloths are particularly fine. ✎ *GC191 • Map F4*

Top 10 Souvenirs

1 Knives

Naifes (traditional long-bladed knives) are still made by hand in Gáldar and Santa Maria de Guía.

2 Lacework and Embroidery

Buy embroidered tablecloths, pretty place mats and blouses in Ingenio.

3 Pottery

The only Guanche tradition to have survived is hand-crafted ceramics. Potters still make their wares without a wheel in La Atalaya, Hoya de Pineda and Juncalillo.

4 Mojo

Take home at least two jars of the spicy sauce: one green and one red *(see p61)*.

5 Timples

This small, five-stringed instrument resembles a ukulele and is the musical emblem of the island. A few artisans still make it by hand.

6 Honey Rum

If the dark rum is too hard to swallow, go for a bottle of this smooth, sweet liquor.

7 Pintaderas

Necklaces of replica Guanche *pintaderas* (ceramic stamps) make an original gift.

8 Agaete Coffee

Strong coffee, grown in the Agaete Valley, is on sale across the island.

9 Aloe Vera

The healing plant grows in abundance on the island, so Gran Canaria is a great place to stock up on cosmetics made from its extracts.

10 Traditional Costume

You'll probably never wear it but the traditional island dress is interesting visually and makes a good wall hanging.

Left **Cuartel de El Colmenar, Valsequillo** Right **Casa de Colón, Las Palmas**

TOP 10 Historical Buildings

Gabinete Literario, Las Palmas

1 Gabinete Literario, Las Palmas

The grand façade grabs your attention, but you have to step inside this Modernist masterpiece to appreciate its splendour. The interior is lavishly decked out in finest Renaissance style, setting it apart from other buildings in the capital. Once the location of the city's first theatre, it is now home to an upmarket cultural centre. *Plaza de Cairasco • Map L5*

2 Casa de los Quintana, Santa María de Guía

Only the presence of a goat and a plate of *gofio* could make this house look more Canarian. A small dragon tree marks the picturesque 17th-century structure, with its superlative balcony. Home of the town's first mayor, it bears his family shield. *Plaza Mayor de Guía • Map C1*

3 Castillo de la Luz

The island's oldest and best example of military architecture dates from the mid-16th century and played an important role in warding off pirate attacks. *Map Q1*

Castillo de la Luz

4 Heredad de Aguas, Arucas

Without their sophisticated irrigation system, the inhabitants of Arucas would not have enjoyed the prosperity they did during the sugar cane years. These days bananas are the main crop, but the water channels are no less important, so it's fitting that the water board should have such grand headquarters. Completed in the early 20th century, the building is topped by an elegant dome. *C/La Heredad 1 • Map D2*

5 Cuartel de El Colmenar, Valsequillo

Originally a cavalry barracks, this fine example of Canarian architecture, built in 1530, is a contender for the title of Gran Canaria's oldest building. *Colmenar Bajo • Map E3*

6 Casa Condal, Juan Grande

A popular events venue, there's no denying the splendour of the Count of Vega Grande's former home. Dating back to the 16th century, the low, whitewashed house is topped by a red-tiled roof. Next door there is a church, built around the same time; recent renovations have restored it to its former glory. *GC500 • Map E5*

7 Teatro Pérez Galdós, Las Palmas

Little remains of the original 19th-century structure, which was almost completely destroyed by fire. Today's theatre is the result of an early 21st-century restoration project by architects Marcos Roger Berghänel and Carlos Díaz. ✆ *Plaza de Stagno 1 • Map M5 • www.teatroperezgaldos.es*

8 Windmills, La Aldea de San Nicolás

On the road from the old town to the coast, there are two fine windmills, built in the 19th century and now restored. The water mill on the road to Artenara is still in working order and boasts a delightful *casa rural*. ✆ *Map B3*

Windmill, La Aldea de San Nicolás

9 Casa de los Patronos de la Virgen, Teror

A pristine example of Canarian architecture, complete with interior patio and rickety wooden balconies *(see p20)*.

10 Casa de Colón, Las Palmas

Although heavily restored, this exquisite building does reveal traces of its 15th-century roots. In the 1940s, several houses were joined and remodelled in finest Neo-Canarian style, creating a home for the Christopher Columbus museum *(see pp8–9)*.

Top 10 Modern Buildings

1 Auditorio Alfredo Kraus, Las Palmas

Oscar Tusquets' beachfront masterpiece *(see p65)*.

2 Palacio de Congresos, Maspalomas

The cube that looks ready to fall off this circular glass edifice is an important conference centre. ✆ *Plaza de las Convenciones • Map D6*

3 Iglesia del Sagrado Corazón de Jesus, Balos

Its asymmetrical roof and monochrome stained glass are highly untraditional. ✆ *Map E4*

4 Police Station, Las Palmas

Locals either love or loathe this multi-coloured tower. ✆ *C/Alcalde José Ramírez Bethencourt • Map J4*

5 El Muelle, Las Palmas

Award-winning Modernist mall opened in 2003 *(see p69)*.

6 AC Hotel, Las Palmas

By night, lights illuminate this 13-storey, cylindrical hotel. ✆ *C/Eduardo Benot 3 • Map P2*

7 Urbanización Turística, Puerto de Mogán

White bougainvillea-draped tourist complex. ✆ *Map B5*

8 Gobierno de Canarias, Las Palmas

This pleasing structure fits in well with its surroundings. ✆ C/ León y Castillo 57 • *Map H3*

9 Biblioteca Pública del Estado, Las Palmas

Agreeably asymmetrical, this library was built in 2002. ✆ Avda Marítima • *Map K5*

10 Cabildo Insular, Las Palmas

The island's finest example of Spanish rationalist architecture ✆ *C/Bravo Murillo • Map L4*

Left **Restaurante Jardín Canario, Tafira Alta** Right **Restaurante Tagoror, Barranco de Guayadeque**

Top 10 Restaurants

1 Restaurante Tagoror, Barranco de Guayadeque

Although it is on the tourist trail, Tagoror's food remains true to its origins, and its prices are low. A series of tunnels connects the rooms, all hewn out of the mountainside. Every Canarian favourite graces the menu: try *gofio*, local *chorizo* sausage, or goat's meat stew. *Montaña Las Tierras 21 • Map E4 • 928 17 20 13 • €€*

Restaurante El Oroval, Agüimes

2 Restaurante Jardín Canario, Tafira Alta

Overlooking the botanical gardens *(see pp14–15)*, this up-market restaurant turns Canarian cuisine into a gourmet affair. *Jardín Botánico Viera y Clavijo (top entrance, on GC110) • Map E2 • 928 35 52 45 • €€€*

3 Dedo de Dios, Puerto de las Nieves

Expect fantastic fresh seafood at this restaurant. Ask for a window table and enjoy the sea views with your fishy meal. Reserve at weekends. *Puerto de las Nieves 10 • Map B2 • 928 89 85 81 • Closed Tue • €€*

4 De Cuchara, Las Palmas

A refreshing mix of Canarian classics is served alongside national, and even international, dishes at this family-run joint. Desserts include the local *huevos mole*, an exceedingly sweet take on meringue. *C/ Alfredo L Jones 37 • Map P2 • 928 26 55 09 • Closed Mon • €€€*

5 Casa Fernando, Soria

In true entrepreneurial style, Casa Fernando's owners have adapted their garage to house this quaint restaurant, stunningly located next to the Presa de Soria. The emphasis is on hearty meals at good prices. All the Canarian favourites feature, such as a superb *ropa vieja*. *Presa de Soria • Map C4 • 928 17 23 46 • Closed Sun • €*

6 Restaurante El Oroval, Agüimes

Agüimes is a charming town and it deserves a restaurant as good as this one, based in the Hotel Casa de los Camellos. Alongside kid meat, rabbit and *carajacas* (chopped liver in a tasty sauce), there are some more familiar choices, such as fresh fish, grilled vegetables, and locally produced cheeses. The desserts are famous among the locals. *C/El Progresso 12 • Map E4 • 928 78 50 03 • Closed Mon • €€€*

Asador Grill de Yolanda, Cruz de Tejeda

For a guide to restaurant price ranges **See p71**

7 Asador Grill de Yolanda, Cruz de Tejeda

;ome here for the friendliest ervice on the island and for ne huge servings of meat. he rustic interior is welcoming, specially in winter. Try the sweet lood-sausage croquettes, a house peciality and much tastier than ney sound. *Cruz de Tejeda • Map 3 • 928 66 62 76 • €€€*

8 Restaurant El Puertillo, El Puertilllo

his restaurant serves the freshest sh dishes. Enjoy the croquetas de ofio y berros (cornmeal and water-ress croquettes) along with Hormi-a family's hospitality. *Paseo de El 'uertillo • Map D1 • 928 62 75 377 • €€€*

asa de Galicia, Las Palmas

9 Casa de Galicia, Las Palmas

ierving Galician seafood pecialities such as oysters and ctopus, Casa de Galicia is one f the best fish restaurants in ne capital. Save room for the lmond tart dessert. *C/Salvador 'uyás 8 • Map P2 • 928 27 98 55 • €€€*

10 Acaymo, Mogán

Don't let the tacky exterior ut you off a kitchen that is opular with the locals as well s with tourists. Stunning views ccompany the delicious meals. he *potaje* is recommended. *El Tostador 23 • Map B4 • 928 56 92 3 • Closed Sun D • €€*

Top 10 Dishes

1 Ropa Vieja

Originally a way to use up leftovers, this chickpea (garbanzo) stew is now a firm favourite among Canarios.

2 Papas Arrugadas

The ubiquitous side order: small potatoes boiled in their skins in very salty water.

3 Mojo

Spicy sauces, heavy on garlic, once used to hide the taste of bad food. The red sauce usually goes with meat and potatoes, while the green version accompanies fish.

4 Gofio

A blend of roasted maize, barley or wheat, served in a variety of ways. Probably the only food surviving from Guanche times, and something of an acquired taste.

5 Bienmesabe

An exceptionally sweet sauce, containing almonds, honey and sugar, that is often eaten with ice cream. The name is also given to a cake with the same ingredients.

6 Potaje de Berros

Stew made with watercress, vegetables and sometimes meat. All Canarians have their own recipe.

7 Queso de Flor

Goat's or sheep's cheese blended with the blue thistle flower; a speciality of Guía.

8 Chorizo de Teror

Locals love sandwiches made with this exceedingly garlicky sausage.

9 Carne de Cabra

The staple meat of the Guanche diet, goat is still a favourite on Canarian menus.

10 Bizcocho

Light, fluffy sponge cake, or sometimes a crispy version.

For more restaurant listings **See pp71, 79, 85, 91 and 99**

AROUND GRAN CANARIA

Left **Playa de Las Canteras** Right **Auditorio Alfredo Kraus**

Las Palmas

LAS PALMAS CAN DATE ITS BEGINNINGS *from the day Juan Rejón landed at La Isleta and earmarked the area for his settlement* (see p34). *Early development was slow, but the arrival of Christopher Columbus, the increase in maritime traffic, and finally the construction of the port, guaranteed success as a trading hub. Today Las Palmas is the Canary Islands' biggest city and, although it shares the title of capital of the archipelago with neighbouring Santa Cruz de Tenerife, the latter lacks the atmosphere of a busy metropolis. The city's ethnic mix reflects its position as a crossroads between Africa, Europe and Latin America. Traditionally dressed Moroccan men suck on hookah pipes while South Americans and northern Europeans socialize nearby. A paradise for shopaholics, Las Palmas also has leafy suburbs and quiet cobbled streets, all crowned by Playa de Las Canteras, one of the world's top city beaches.*

Las Palmas at night

Top 10 Sights

1. Playa de Las Canteras
2. Auditorio Alfredo Kraus
3. Casa de Colón
4. Catedral de Santa Ana
5. Guagua Turística
6. Museo Elder de la Ciencia y la Tecnología
7. Triana
8. Museo Néstor
9. Vegueta Architecture
10. Museo Canario

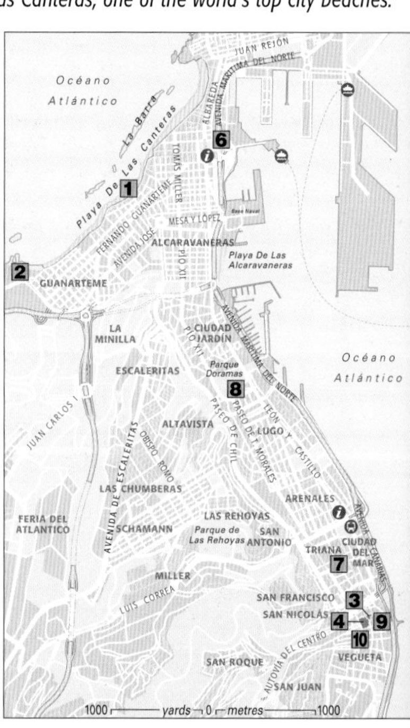

 Preceding pages **Playa de Las Canteras, Las Palmas**

1 Playa de Las Canteras

Few cities can boast a beach as good as this: 3 km (2 miles) of fine sand, sandwiched between a wide promenade and the chilly Atlantic Ocean. Surfers congregate at the western end, an area known as La Cicer. The sand here is black, but moving eastward it gets ever more golden, and the sea, protected by the broad reef, takes on the appearance of a lake. Locals sometimes head for *el ascensor* ("the lift"), a part of the reef where the swell catapults swimmers back up onto the rocks – look for the throng of whooping youngsters in front of Playa Chica. *Map N2*

2 Auditorio Alfredo Kraus

One of the city's landmark buildings, this fine modern auditorium, perched on the jetty at the western end of Playa de Las Canteras, hosts cultural events, including the opera season, the film festival and jazz concerts. Should the show not inspire, there's a stunning ocean view. *Avda Príncipe de Asturias s/n • Map G3 • 928 49 17 70 • www.auditorio-alfredokraus.com• Guided tours are available for groups • Adm charge*

3 Casa de Colón

The main focus of this first-rate museum is Christopher Columbus's travels across the Atlantic and their effect on the Canary Islands. Pre-Columbian cultures and historic Las Palmas are rewarding subsidiary themes. It's all displayed in a restored Canarian house *(see pp8–9)*.

Catedral de Santa Ana

4 Catedral de Santa Ana

The enormous cathedral and adjoining sacred art museum contain some important paintings and sculptures, including two works by local sculptor José Luján Pérez *(see pp10–11)*.

5 Guagua Turística

The open-top double-decker may have originated in London, but Gran Canaria certainly has the climate for it. The hop-on, hop-off tour departs from Parque Sta Catalina and takes in Castillo de la Luz, Avda Mesa y López, the Alfredo Kraus auditorium, Parque Doramas, Avda Marítima, and the upper part of the city for its fine views *(see p68)*. Vegueta's streets are too narrow for the bus, but there's a stop nearby so you can explore it at your leisure. An excellent way to see the whole city in a day. *Parque Sta Catalina • Map P3 • 928 30 58 00 • http://www.city-sightseeing.com/en/tours/spain/las-palmas-de-gran-canaria.htm • 9:30am–5:30pm daily (buses depart every 30 mins) • Adm charge • No disabled access*

Casa Museo de Colón

In summer, a large cloud known as the "panza de burro" ("donkey's belly") hangs over the city, so it's warm but rarely sunny.

Free Trade

Ever since Puerto de La Luz was built, it has been a free port; indeed, low taxes, lenient customs laws and strategic location combine to make it one of the world's busiest, handling nearly 7 million tonnes of goods a year. The bustling docks give the city its cosmopolitan feel, as Russian and Korean sailors rub shoulders with European cruise passengers.

6 Museo Elder de la Ciencia y la Tecnología

While kids enjoy the many interactive exhibits, parents might prefer to find out how beer is made, what they would weigh on Mars, or if their hearing and heartbeat are normal. This is a fine place to spend a few hours, especially if you're caught in the rain in Las Palmas. *Parque Santa Catalina • Map P2 • 828 011 828 • www.museoelder.org • 10am–8pm Tue–Sun • Adm charge*

7 Triana

Not long after the Conquest, the original Vegueta settlement became too small for the island's increasing population and spread across the Guiniguada ravine. By the 19th century, the neighbouring district of Triana was a bustling area, boasting some fine architecture and a large theatre. It was formerly the elite that shopped on the city's premiere street, Calle Mayor de Triana, but these days, affordable chain stores complement the exclusive boutiques. Do venture away from the main street, for it is in the side streets that you will find Triana's treasures – such as one-off handicraft shops and snug *tapas* bars. There's more to Triana than shopping: admire the exquisite architecture of the Gabinete Literario and the Teatro Pérez Galdós *(see pp58–9)*, and also the Ermita de San Telmo *(see p39)*.

Calle Mayor de Triana

Museo Néstor

8 Museo Néstor

Las Palmas-born artist Néstor Martín Fernández de la Torre is best known as a Modernist painter, but you can also see evidence of Pre-Raphaelitism and Symbolism in his colourful works. Construction of the Neo-Canarian building housing the gallery was a joint project by the artist and his architect brother Miguel. As well as Néstor's famous "poems", huge paintings comprising eight panels each, don't miss the vivid sketches based on theatre productions. Towards the end of his life, he favoured pictures depicting hidden corners of his beloved Gran Canaria, in a style he called "Typism" *(see also*

'egueta architecture, Plaza del Espíritu Santo

›36). Pueblo Canario • Map J4 • 928 '4 51 35 • www.laspalmasgc.es/mnostor. om • 10am–7pm Tue–Sat, 10:30am– :30pm Sun and public hols • Adm charge

9 Vegueta Architecture

A stroll around the capital's ıldest district is a must for its uiet cobbled streets and varied rchitecture. Unfortunately, pirate ttacks in the 16th century estroyed much of the original amlet set up after the Conquest, ut there is still plenty to see. alconies prevail, be they the neven wooden-box-like designs ıvoured in Canarian architecture r the more ornate wrought-iron ersions typical of Modernist uildings. Of course, the centre-iece of the *barrio* (district) is ıe cathedral *(see pp10–11)*, but ɔn't limit your viewing to this ıammoth construction. *Map M5*

0 Museo Canario

This museum boasts the rgest collection of Guanche rtifacts to be found anywhere nd gives a fascinating insight ıto their culture. This is a good reparation for those who may e visiting Guanche sites around ıe island *(see pp12–13)*.

Las Palmas Past and Present

Morning

Any walk around the capital should begin where *it* did, in the Vegueta *barrio*. Start at the **Palacio de Justicia**, on Avda Marítima, and head into the old town via a narrow alley to the right of the courts; just a 17th-century tower remains of the original building. Pass the impressive stone archway of the Jesuit Iglesia de San Francisco de Borja as you make your way to the must-see **Museo Canario**.

From the museum, head to the **Plaza and Ermita de Espíritu Santo**, then double back again to the **cathedral**. Behind it are the wonderful **Casa de Colón** and **Ermita de San Antonio Abad**. There are two superb restaurants here, Cho Zacariás and Casa Montesdeoca; or for a cheap lunch, head to the busy Mercado de Vegueta.

Afternoon

After lunch, cross to C/Mayor de Triana to shop for souvenirs and clothes, and admire the striking houses. Head north to San Telmo Park, where there's a bus station. Here you can jump on a *guagua* to cross the city, unless you relish the idea of a 45-minute stroll along the promenade. Alight at Avda José Mesa y López if you want to visit the El Corte Inglés store.

Plazoleta de Farray is a popular square for a coffee, beer or a plate of *tapas*. From here, it's a stone's throw to the beach via C/Kant. Get a home-made ice cream from Peña la Vieja and join the locals ambling along in the *paseo*.

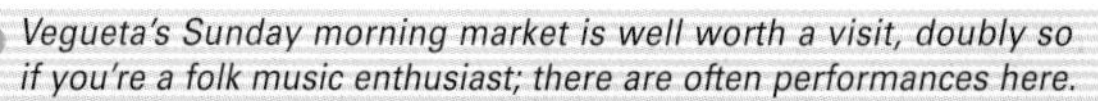

Vegueta's Sunday morning market is well worth a visit, doubly so if you're a folk music enthusiast; there are often performances here.

Left **Casa Museo Pérez Galdós** Right **Pueblo Canario**

TOP 10 Best of the Rest

1 Playa de las Alcaravaneras
Its location next to the port might put swimmers off, but the lack of sunbathers makes this a popular place to practise aquatic sports such as sailing. *Map J3*

2 Casa Museo Pérez Galdós
Novelist Benito Pérez Galdós – "the Spanish Charles Dickens" – is the island's most famous son. His charming childhood home in Triana is now a museum. *C/ Cano 2 • Map L5 • 928 36 69 76 • www.casamuseoperezgaldos.com • 10am–2pm, 4–8pm Tue–Fri, 10am–2pm Sat–Sun (guided tours only, every hour) • Free*

3 Castillo de la Luz
The 16th-century fort overlooks a popular children's playground. Set in a small park equipped with a cheap café serving tasty food, it's also a fine place to wile away an afternoon. *C/Juan Rejón s/n • Map Q1*

4 Las Coloradas
Enjoy a seafood lunch in this *barrio* north of Las Canteras, worlds away from the bustle of the city. Wander up the mountain for a superlative view of the isthmus. *Map E1*

5 Parque Doramas
The city's prettiest park is named after the brave Guanche leader who refused to bow down to the Spanish. It's well equipped for children, and there's a small open-air café for parents. *C/Emilio Ley • Map J4*

6 CAAM
From outside, the Centro Atlántico de Arte Moderno is jus another Neo-Classical building. Inside, Vegueta's most modern space is host to contemporary sculptures, paintings and audio-visual artworks. *C/Los Balcones 1 • Map M5 • 928 31 18 00 • www.caam.ne • 10am–9pm Tue–Sat, 10am–2pm Sun • Fre*

7 Vistas from Escaleritas
You'll get the best view of the city in all its variety – port, beaches, skyscrapers, mansions and palm trees – from the Escaleritas *barrio*. *Map H4*

8 Muelle Deportivo
The sporting marina attracts sailors from across the globe – often to rest before heading to southern Africa or across the Atlantic. *Map J3*

9 Ciudad Jardín
As you enter "Garden City", the unsightly skyscrapers of Las Palmas's commercial districts suddenly give way to grand mansions, mostly built by Britisl settlers in the 19th and early 20t centuries and now home to the city's wealthiest families. *Map H*

10 Pueblo Canario
Built in the mid-20th centur this miniature Canarian village is a good place to sample local cuisin buy handicrafts or admire the wor of Néstor de la Torre *(see p36)*. *C/Francisco González Díaz • Map J4 • 10am–midnight Tue–Sat, 10:30am–5pm S*

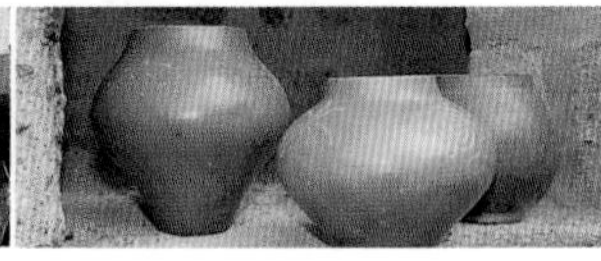

eft **El Corte Inglés** Right **FEDAC**

10 Places to Shop

1 Calle Mayor de Triana

Although Avda de Mesa y López is vying for the position of op shopping street, Triana still has the charm. *Map L4*

2 El Corte Inglés

If you can't find what you're ooking for in this mammoth department store, it may well not exist! There are two branches on Avda de José Mesa y López and a hird in the 7 Palmas shopping centre. *Map P3*

3 FEDAC

The best artisans from across he island unite to sell their wares n this government-run outlet in Triana. It's a non-profit organiation, so you know your euro is going straight to the craftsmen. *C/Domingo J Navarro 7 • Map L4*

4 Artesanía Santa Catalina

This is a good place to hunt or typical Canarian souvenirs. Their speciality is pottery, but ou will also find foodstuffs, aloe era products and embroidered goods. *C/Ripoche 4 • Map P3*

5 La Librería

Every aspect of Canarian culture, from hiking and history to festivals and flora, s represented in the *cabildo*'s bookshop in Triana. Although most titles are in Spanish, a ew have been translated into other European languages for hose who want to delve deeper. *C/Cano 24 • Map L4*

6 Tienda Artesania Canaria Las Palmitas

The perfect place to pick up an interesting souvenir or gift, while at the same time supporting local artisans. The shop is crammed with handicrafts from wooden jewellery to earthenware jugs. *C/Herrería 7, Vegueta • Map M5*

7 Malls

Las Palmas has no less than seven shopping malls. *La Ballena: C/General del Norte 112. Map G6 • 7 Palmas: Avda Pintor Felo Monzón s/n (off map) • Monopol: Plaza de Hurtado Mendoza 1. Map L5 • El Muelle: Muelle de Santa Catalina. Map P2 • Las Arenas: C/Pavía 12. Map G3 • La Minilla: C/Pintor Juan Guillermo 6–8. Map H3 • Tamarana: Avda César Manrique s/n (off map)*

8 Calle Ripoche

If you're looking for a cheap replica of traditional Canarian dress, head to this street near Parque Santa Catalina. It might not be truly authentic, but this is where the locals buy their gear for the *romerías*. *Map P3*

9 Idiomátika

This shop specializes in foreign-language books. *C/Senador Castillo Olivares 52. Map J5 • Plazoleta de Farray 1. Map H2 • El Muelle. Map P2*

10 El Puente

This charming shop stocks typical Canarian crafts such as tablecloths, pottery and traditional Canarian costumes. *C/Obispo Codina 6 • Map L5*

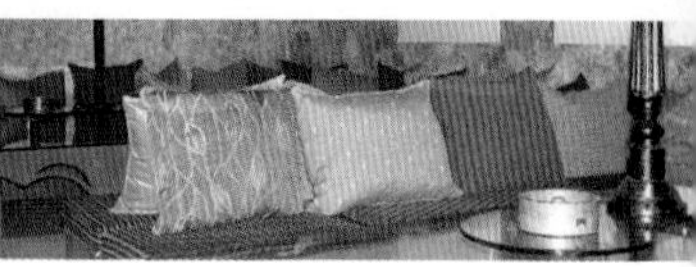

Left **Teatro Cuyás** Right **Las Brujas**

TOP 10 Nightspots

1 Fortuni
With its retro design and contemporary styling, this venue in the heart of the capital has certainly made a name for itself. Expect live singers, top DJs and some pretty crazy party nights throughout the year. *C/Martinez de Escobar 1 • Map H2*

2 Charleston Café
Acoustic concerts and absinthe gives this late-night café a Bohemian air, which attracts a relaxed crowd. *C/Buenos Aires 14 • Map L4*

3 Teatro Cuyás
If you want an earlier, quieter night out, try this modern theatre. Plays are always in Spanish, but there are live music events as well, and a wonderful restaurant serving creative cuisine. *C/Viera y Clavijo s/n • Map L4*

4 Cuasquías
The high ceilings and spacious rooms are a breath of fresh air. Catch a live band playing jazz or Latin music at weekends from 1am, or enjoy a game of pool. *C/San Pedro 2 • Map M5*

5 Tao Club & Garden
Not one for ravers, Tao has a chill-out lounge (the club) and a restaurant (the garden). Choose one of the delicious cocktails, find a comfy sofa and relax to the ambient sounds. *Jardines Alonso Quesada s/n • Map J3*

6 Treinta y Tantos
As the name suggests (*treinta* means "thirty"), the clientele here are largely in their thirties. Local bands play Spanish and international hits, mostly from the 70s and 80s; a DJ fills in the breaks with more retro classics. *C/José Franchy Roca • Map P3*

7 Pool Fiction
Equipped with eight pool tables, a dartboard and a plasma TV, this sophisticated joint behind Prague Santa Catalina is ideal for a sporting night out. *C/Secretario Artiles 22 • Map P3*

8 Las Brujas
Outside the city on the way to Tafira, a huge rural house has been converted into an amazing nightspot. You can wander around, or stop for a bite to eat in one of the small dining rooms dotted about the house. In summer, revellers spill out into the garden. *Barranco Seco • Map E2*

9 Paper Club
Once La Floridita, a favourite of the oldies, it has now transformed into one of Las Palmas' best concert venues. *C/Remedios 10–12 • Map L5*

10 Malecón de la Habana
This is one of the best places in the city to hear Latin music, dance to the rhythm of salsa and watch live Cuban bands. Hots up around 3am. *C/José Franchy Roca • Map P3*

Few clubs demand a cover charge, but you may have to buy a ticket for a drink on entry.

Casa Montesdeoca

Price Categories

For a three-course meal for one with half a bottle of wine (or equivalent meal), taxes and extra charges.	
€	under €20
€€	€20–€30
€€€	€30–€40
€€€€	€40–€50
€€€€€	over €50

Top 10 Places to Eat

1 Rías Bajas

The capital's premier restaurant specializes in seafood. If you're daunted by the choice, try the *paella* or the *arroz caldoso*, a kind of rice stew with a multitude of seafood. *C/Simón Bolívar 3 • Map P2 • 928 27 13 16 • €€€€€*

2 Casa de Galicia

Another wonderful place to sample seafood and fish, along with its adjoining sister restaurant El Arrosar. Try the *arroz negro* (black rice) cooked in squid ink – simply delicious. *C/Salvador Cuyás 8 • Map P2 • 928 27 98 55 • €€€€*

3 Tehran

Tehran offers an authentic Iranian experience in terms of cuisine, costumes, Persian decor and even cultural entertainment. *C/Bernando de la Torre 1 • Map N3 • 928 22 28 17 • €€€*

4 De Tapa en Tapa

Settle into one of the cosy wooden booths and choose from a superb selection of *tapas*. Recommended: the spicy *papa bomba*; dates wrapped in bacon; courgette omelette. *C/Diderot 23 • Map N3 • 928 49 00 55 • Closed Sun • €*

5 Chacalote

A meal at this welcoming seafood restaurant adorned with nautical paraphernalia feels more like eating in a small fishing village than a hectic metropolis. *C/Proa 3 • Map F2 • San Cristóbal • 928 31 21 40 • €€€*

6 Galia

Excellent French food in a romantic setting. Enjoy game dishes you won't find anywhere else on the island, such as wild boar, venison and ostrich. *C/Luis Morote 49 • Map P2 • 928 22 32 19 • Closed Sun, bank holidays • €€€€€*

7 Restaurante Asador El Cid

Popular with visitors and locals, this rustic eatery serves a mean roast suckling pig, Segovian-style. *C/Nicolás Estévanez 10 • Map P3 • 928 22 46 31 • €€€*

8 Fuji

Gran Canaria's first Japanese restaurant, Fuji offers authentic dishes and friendly service. You'll need to reserve a table at the weekend to indulge in the delicious sushi and sashimi. *C/ Fernando Guanarteme 56 • Map N3 • 928 26 13 93 • Closed Mon • €€€€*

9 La Alquitara

Unusual dishes such as kangaroo steak accompany a select *tapas* menu. There's an excellent-value three-course *menu del día* and an extensive wine list. *C/Domingo J Navarro 9 • Map L4 • 928 38 49 59 • €€€*

10 Casa Montesdeoca

Succulent steaks and fresh fish are followed by some unique home-made desserts at this atmospheric restaurant, carefully restored in traditional Vegueta style. *C/Montesdeoca 10 • Map M5 • 928 33 34 66 • Closed Sun, Aug • €€€€*

For more restaurant listings **See pp60–61, 79, 85, 91 and 99**

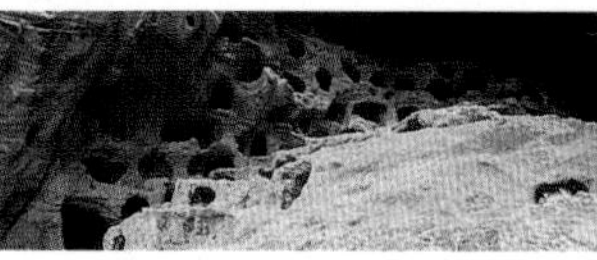

Left **Cenobio de Valerón** Right **Natural pools, Dos Roques**

Northern Gran Canaria

THE NORTH IS AS FAR REMOVED *from the stereotype of the Canary Islands as is possible. The humid climate here blesses the ravines with a layer of rich green vegetation, while rough seas crash against the stony beaches. It's not dream territory for sunbathers or swimmers, but hikers and surfers are certainly well catered for. The less energetic can enjoy a satisfying culinary experience, either sampling warming meat dishes in the highlands, or tucking into a seafood platter on the coast. The region is also rich in pre-Hispanic history and aboriginal remains, since Gáldar was the island's capital before the Europeans invaded.*

Top 10 Sights

1. Puerto de las Nieves
2. Cueva Pintada, Gáldar
3. Casa Museo Antonio Padrón, Gáldar
4. Cenobio de Valerón
5. Los Tilos de Moya
6. Parroquia de Nuestra Señora de la Candelaria, Moya
7. Santa María de Guía, Old Quarter
8. Parroquia de San Juan Bautista
9. Valle de Agaete
10. Natural Pools

View of Puerto de las Nieves

Preceding pages **The golf course at Caldera de Bandama**

1 Puerto de las Nieves

The increasing number ' visitors fails to sap the ıaracter of the north's vourite fishing village. ettle into the slow pace of e here, and enjoy a divine eafood grill overlooking the ɔrt *(see pp30–31).*

Town house in Puerto de las Nieves

2 Cueva Pintada, Gáldar

'hen a farmer from Gáldar disɔvered a Guanche cave under s land in the 19th century, he ɔuld not have realized the magtude of his find. Archeologists ıoved in to study the simple aintings adorning its walls – nall triangles and squares ched in shades of red and own. These soon became garded as the most important et of Guanche engravings in istence, but humidity and ıman contact began to destroy em. The site was closed in the 970s while the problem was ckled; it has now opened to the ıblic. ✎ *C/Audencia 2, ildar • Map C1 • 928 89 89 (book in advance) www.cuevapintada.org*

Cueva Pintada

3 Casa Museo Antonio Padrón, áldar

ɔrn in Gáldar in 1920, Antonio ıdrón was known as an pressionist painter, though s work also shows Fauvist ndencies. He portrayed everyday ınarian life, often focusing on cal myths, customs and folklore. ıdrón's most familiar works – gether with some paintings ɔm the 1960s which he later jected – are displayed in his rmer studio. ✎ *C/Drago 2 • Map C1 928 551 858 • www.antoniopadron.com am–3pm Mon–Fri • Free*

4 Cenobio de Valerón

It's not uncommon to see grain stores on Guanche sites, but none comes close to the Cenobio de Valerón. Located in a cave, this early version of a pantry consists of over 300 hollows, whittled out of the rock face. Although access is easy today, the Cenobio was built on an inaccessible crag, to keep food supplies out of the way of thieves. The early theory that the site was a convent, where young girls lived a life of celibacy away from society, has long since been discarded. ✎ *GC291 km 21 • Map D1 • www.cenobiodevaleron.com • Oct–Mar: 10am–5pm Tue–Sun; Apr–Sep: 10am–6pm Tue–Sun • Adm charge (free for children below 10)*

5 Los Tilos de Moya

Gran Canaria's only natural laurel forest may not be as impressive as those found on other Macronesian islands, but the misty trees are an ideal spot for a hike or picnic. The Canaries' biggest expanse of laurel forest is in La Gomera's national park. Los Tilos de Moya represents about one per cent of the once magnificent Doramas forest. Home to many endangered bird and plant species, it has only a sprinkling of human inhabitants. ✎ *Access via GC70 and GC703 • Map D2*

Parroquia de Nuestra Señora de la Candelaria, Moya

6 Parroquia de Nuestra Señora de la Candelaria, Moya

Clinging precariously to the side of the Moya ravine, this church must have been built by brave workmen. Completed in 1957, it is a pleasingly higgledy-piggledy blend of towers and roofs of varying heights. The best views are from the GC700 road from Guía. *Padre Juanito 9 • Map D2 • 928 620 007 • 6–8pm Mon–Sat, 11am–noon, 6–8pm Sun • Free*

7 Santa María de Guía, Old Quarter

At first glance, Guía has little to offer other than a hotchpotch of modern buildings just off a busy motorway. Yet, hidden away in the centre of this sprawl stands a grand Neo-Classical church and one of the island's most charming town centre[s]. The church, begun in 1607, has a clock donated by celebrate[d] sculptor José Luján Pérez, Guía's most famous son. His hom[e], marked by a small plaque, is in a pretty road behind the churc[h]. These sleepy, colourf[ul] streets ooze characte[r] and the inhabitants a[re] perhaps the friendlie[st] on the island. *Map*

Water Channels

Rainfall is far higher in the north, but as the porous ground soaks it up, farmers have had to build irrigation channels, wells, springs and water mills. This impressive hydro-network supports the cultivation of crops in the region, particularly the banana plantations around Arucas. The area's hydraulic heritage can be seen on a hike around Valleseco.

8 Parroquia de San Juan Bautista, Arucas

For centuries a small chapel wa[s] enough to satisfy the spiritual needs of Arucas's citizens. As the town became more prosperous, the population grew and the faithful demanded a larger place of worship. In 1909 the old hermitage was demolished to make way for th[e] current church, a mammoth Neo-Gothic structure. Construction took over 60 years but the locals agree that it was worth the wait for what is certainly the most remarkable church in Gran Canaria. The exquisite stained-glass window[s] were produced in the 1920s by French designers Maumejean e[t] Frères and are considered the best on the island. *Párroco Cardenes 2 • Map D2 • 928 605 622 9:30am–12:30pm, 4:30–7pm Mon–Sat 8:30am–1pm, 4:30–7:30pm Sun • Free*

9 Valle de Agaete

So far, even the finest engineers have failed to link th[e] Agaete Valley with the centre o[f] the island, the steep Tamadaba precipice forbidding any though[t] of construction. After snaking along the valley, passing remot[e] hamlets dotted here and there,

e road fizzles out just after Los errezales. Fruit orchards and offee plantations fill the valley oor, while the Tamadaba pine orest provides a formidable ackdrop, towering hundreds of etres overhead. There is a agnificent hike on a well-arked path all the way to rtenara, but the walk is more anageable if you start at the ther end. *GC231 from Agaete town entre • Map C2*

nar de Tamadaba, Valle de Agaete

Natural Pools

Since the north coast is con-dered dangerous for swimmers, wn councils have given nature helping hand, building pools at are constantly replenished y the sea. Locals favour the large *scinas* at Bañaderos, close to e capital, though those further ong the coast offer a more anquil swim. The pools at San renzo have decent facilities, ut head further west to Roque rieto and Dos Roques for less-sited spots. Beware that even the pools, waves and currents n still be a little overpowering high tide. *Bañaderos: Map D1 San Lorenzo: Map D1 • Roque Prieto: ap C1 • Dos Roques: Map C1*

A Culinary Trek

Morning

If the best way to get to know a place is through its cuisine, then the north is where you'll discover Gran Canaria. Start the day in **Arucas**, allowing half an hour to visit the Parroquia de San Juan Bautista, before taking a guided tour with free tipple at the Arehucas rum factory. You'll pass a few remote villages along the GC300 before reaching **Firgas**. The unusual town centre has a functioning *gofio* mill, so sampling the most Canarian of all foods *(see p61)* is a must. Head through the Barranco de Azuaje to **Moya**, where all cafés serve local *suspiros* (meringues) and *bizcocho* (crispy sponge cakes).

The road to Guía skirts the Los Tilos laurel forest *(see p75)*, and a worthy detour on the GC291 leads to the **Cenobio de Valerón** *(see p75)*. Walk to this Guanche site and enjoy the verdant views. From here, join the motorway to **Puerto de las Nieves** *(see p75)*, the ideal spot for a fishy lunch.

Afternoon

Backtrack along the GC1 to **Gáldar**, home of the Cueva Pintada and the Casa Museo Antonio Padrón *(see p75)*. Cross the motorway to **Santa Maria de Guía** to wander through the picturesque old town and buy delicious local cheese. Casa Arturo, on Calle Lomo Guillén, is the best place to buy some *queso de flor (see p61)*, generally considered the island's tastiest cheese. End the day by taking a dip in the popular natural pools at either **San Lorenzo** or **Bañaderos**.

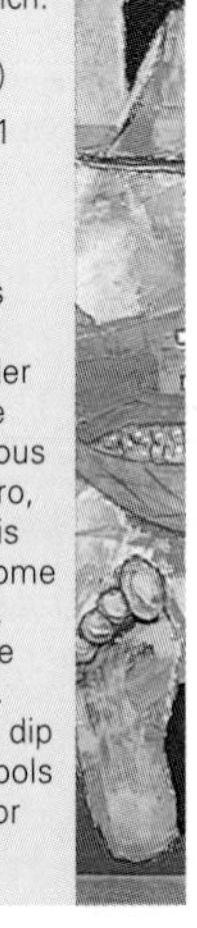

Avoid minor roads in winter months, when heavy rain can cause rocks to fall.

Left **Jardín de la Marquesa** Right **Túmulo de La Guancha**

Top 10 Best of the Rest

1 Jardín de la Marquesa, Arucas

These impressive botanical gardens bordering an ornate 19th-century mansion are home to over 2,500 species of flora, both native and tropical. *GC330, Las Hoyas 2 • Map D2 • 928 60 44 86 • 9am–1pm, 2–6pm Mon–Sat • Adm charge*

2 Rum Factory, Arucas

A brief tour of the factory concludes with a tasting session and a chance to buy at a discount. *Era de San Pedro 2 • Map D2 • 928 62 49 00 • 9am–2pm Mon–Fri • Free*

3 Firgas Town Centre

Often considered dull, Firgas has a charming town centre. The star sight is the mill – see a demonstration and buy a bag of freshly ground *gofio* *(see p61)*. *Map D2*

4 Casa-Museo Tomás Morales, Moya

This museum honours Moya poet Tomás Morales, though for non-Spanish-speakers the interest lies more in seeing inside an upmarket 19th-century home. *Plaza de Tomás Morales • Map D2 • 928 62 02 17 • 10am–8pm Mon–Sun • Free*

5 Hidden Coves

The north coast is not noted for its beaches, but it has some quiet coves if you know where to look. The prettiest are on the Gáldar coast, but Playa Sotavento north of Puerto de las Nieves also deserves a visit. *Map C1, D1, B2*

6 Gáldar Architecture

The unusual church *(see p3* dominates the pretty plaza, but there are other buildings of interest, such as the eclectic Teatro Municipal, the 19th-century casino, and the town ha whose patio houses the island's oldest dragon tree. *Map C1*

7 Túmulo de La Guancha

This huge circular construction is the island's largest burial site, with 42 tombs radiating from one central grave. *Gáldar El Agujero road • Map C1 • 928 21 94 2 ext 4441 • No fixed opening hours; visit by appointment • Free*

8 Huerto de las Flores, Agaete

More than 100 species of tropical plants thrive in this small garden. *C/Huertas • Map C2 • 9am–2pm Mon–Fri • Free*

9 Sardina

The fine sandy beach brings bathers from miles around on sunny weekends, so visit this fishing village midweek if you want to find space to put your towel down. *Map C1*

10 Finca La Laja, Valle de Agaete

This San Pedro estate of unique beauty is well worth the detour, especially for sampling the delicious wine, coffee and the Tropical fruits of Ageate Valley *Map C2 • 628 95 25 88 • Visit by appointment only*

Remember that the seas off the north coast are not suitable for swimming.

Price Categories

For a three-course meal for one with half a bottle of wine (or equivalent meal), taxes and extra charges.

€	under €20
€€	€20–€30
€€€	€30–€40
€€€€	€40–€50
€€€€€	over €50

Marisquería Fragata, Sardina del Norte

Top 10 Places to Eat

1 Marisquería Fragata, Sardina del Norte

Set right on the seafront, this friendly place offers old favourites such as squid and octopus alongside more original choices like gooseneck barnacles. *Avda Antonio Rosas • Map C1 • 928 88 32 96 • Closed Sun D, Wed • €€*

2 Casa Brito, Visvique

Barbecued meats in a cosy rustic setting. Leave space for dessert – the rice pudding *(arroz con leche)* and crêpes are divine. *Pasaje de Ter 17 • Map D2 • 928 62 23 23 • Closed Sun D, Mon, Tue • €€€*

3 Locanda El Roque, El Roque

Eat Italian cuisine at the end of a rock in coastal Moya. It is a culinary experience you will not easily forget. *El Roque 58 • Map D1 • 928 61 00 44 • €€*

4 Restaurante Dedo de Dios, Puerto de las Nieves

This huge seafood restaurant is packed at weekends with lunching families. The fish soup is highly recommended. *Ctra General Muelle Viejo • Map B2 • 928 89 80 00 • Closed Tue • €€*

5 El Mirador Del Atlante, GC2

Try the simply cooked food at this restaurant with a beautiful sea view, overlooked by the El Atlante sculpture on the main northern highway. *Ctra del Rincón • Map E1 • 615 39 12 85 • €€*

6 Las Brasas, Firgas

The barbecued meats and roast chicken attract diners to this no-frills joint where you can fill up on home cooking at low prices. *Avda de la Cruz 36 • Map D2 • 928 62 52 50 • €*

7 La Cueva, Sardina del Norte

In a twist on the usual cave-eating experience, the speciality is fish, not meat. Cheery lighting and soft furnishings lend a warm feel. *Avda Alcalde Antonio Rosas 80 • Map C1 • 928 88 02 36 • Closed Tue in winter • €*

8 Casa Pepe, Agaete

The steaks are good, but the tasty fish soup and freshly caught grilled prawns are what keep the locals coming back. *C/Alcalde de Armas Galván 5 • Map C2 • 928 89 82 27 • Closed Wed • €€*

9 El Cápita, Puerto de las Nieves

Seafood restaurants abound here, but locals insist that this family-run place outclasses the competition. *C/Nuestra Señora de las Nieves 37 • Map B2 • 928 55 41 42 • Closed Mon–Thu D • €€*

10 La Tasquita, Santa María de Guía

Take a dip in the ocean before sampling the catch of the day at this friendly waterfront restaurant. There are alternatives, but it's the fresh fish that brings people back. *C/San Felipe 32 • Map C1 • 928 55 63 83 • Closed Sun D, Mon • €€€*

For more restaurant listings **See pp60–61, 71, 85, 91 and 99**

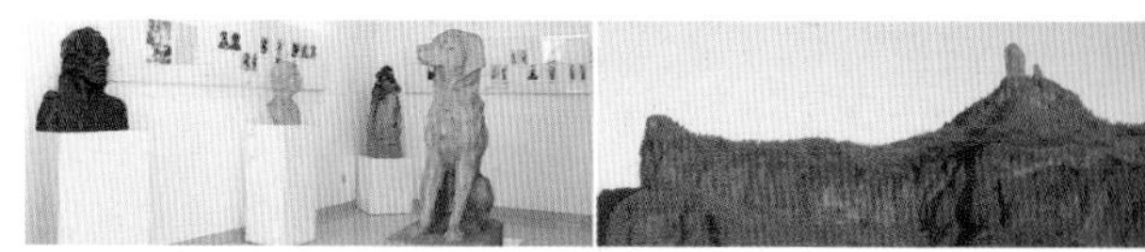

Left **Museo Abraham Cárdenes, Tejeda** Right **Roque Nublo**

Central and Western Gran Canaria

FOR YEARS, THE RUGGED CENTRAL REGION *could be traversed only by a series of tough paths, known as* caminos reales. *Today, hardy hikers continue to trek these old routes, though driving has long since ousted walking as the main way of getting about, however dizzying the roads may be. The west, however, remains largely unvisited and unspoilt. The plunging hollows nature has sliced from the towering cliffs hinder any road construction, meaning that the only way to explore this breathtaking region is on foot. Just three scary stretches of road lead to La Aldea de San Nicolás, the island's remotest* pueblo. *This is a region for enjoying a hike, or dangling a fishing rod lazily into the ocean.*

Top 10 Sights

1. Roque Nublo
2. Pico de las Nieves
3. Roque Bentayga and Cuevas del Rey
4. Pinar de Tamadaba
5. Tejeda
6. Ermita de la Virgen de la Cuevita
7. Cruz de Tejeda
8. Teror
9. Playa de Güigüi
10. Puerto de la Aldea

C/Real de la Plaza, Teror

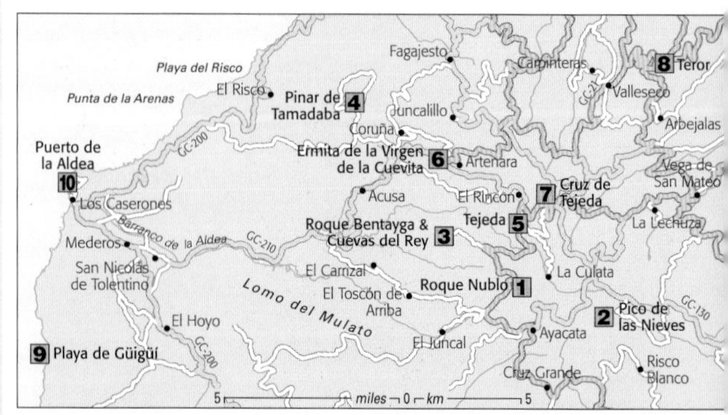

'iew from the summit of Pico de las Nieves

1 Roque Nublo

It's easy to see why the ;uanches revered the looming orm of this 80-m (260-ft) nono-lith, especially when it's een up close *(see p24)*.

2 Pico de las Nieves

The island's highest point aturally offers impressive vistas, f you can only get there before he clouds do. After winter nowfalls, the area is swamped vith islanders wanting to get brief glimpse of the white tuff. The area is also known as 'ozo de las Nieves ("Well of the nows"): nearby, there is an bandoned well once used to ollect snow that was later ransported to the capital to e used in food reservation *see p25)*.

3 Roque Bentayga and Cuevas del Rey

Although best known s a place of worship nd possible royal esidence, this tumpy rock served nother purpose. In prime position for potting unwelcome visitors, Bentayga acted as a stronghold, playing its part in delaying the Conquest, albeit briefly *(see p24)*.

Roque Bentayga

4 Pinar de Tamadaba

The island's largest pine forest offers respite from bustling towns and busy roads. Stop at the picnic area for lunch, or make the 30-minute walk from the Casa Forestal to the area's highest point, at 1,440 m (4,720 ft) *(see pp42)*.

5 Tejeda

The main attraction of this town is its splendid location in the centre of the immense Caldera de Tejeda. This huge depression measures 18 km (11 miles) across. It was described by Spanish poet Miguel de Unamuno as "a tremendous upset of the innards of the earth". As well as the spectacular vistas, there is a small art gallery and two farming museums, Museo de las Tradiciones and Museo Las Tres Cruces *(see p25)*.

Stock up on bottled water before you set off; in this region, shops are scarce.

Ermita de la Virgen de la Cuevita

6 Ermita de la Virgen de la Cuevita

Utilizing the landscape has always been a feature of Canarian life, but few places have maintained the tradition of inhabiting caves. In Artenara, however, people still opt for cave living, and tourists can stay in an adapted grotto. Although the main church is an impressive 19th-century construction, the chapel closest to the hearts of the locals is the simple Ermita de la Virgen de la Cuevita. Gouged out of a cliff face, the chapel lacks the pomp of most Canarian churches, with few religious images other than the statue of the Virgen de la Cuevita ("Madonna of the Little Cave"). It is a rough-and-ready work, outshone by counterparts in other churches, but that does not stop the faithful flocking to worship her. Oddly enough, she is the patron of both cyclists and Canarian folklore groups. To get to the chapel, follow the signs from the main square for the 10-minute uphill walk *(see also p39)*.

Map C3 • No disabled access

Early Christianization

The pre-Hispanic name for the island's westernmost town is unknown, as it had been renamed after an Italian saint long before the conquerors arrived. Mallorcan monks landed on the small beach in 1342, and promptly erected a primitive chapel next to the ocean. Although the area was quite densely populated, when it took on the title San Nicolás de Tolentino, the original name was lost. Sadly, the hermitage was demolished in the 16th century.

7 Cruz de Tejeda

This large, sombre, intricately carved crucifix of grey-green stone marks the notional – though not, in fact, the precise geographical – centre of the island. These days, all roads meet here, but for centuries this was a junction only of the *caminos reales*, the network of "king's highways" that once criss-crossed the island. Most of the paths are still well maintained, and offer dramatic mountain hikes. These include a lush downhill walk to Teror, various routes around the island's centre, and even a tough trek to Puerto de las Nieves on the coast *(see p25)*.

Cruz de Tejeda

8 Teror

This charming and historically important town offers the island's best examples of traditional architecture, as well as an impressive church *(see pp20–23)*.

9 Playa de Güigüí

For those who complain that Gran Canaria's beaches are too built up and crowded, a trip to Güigüí is in order. Its fine, dark sand is flanked by looming cliffs, creating a breathtaking sight. You will have earned your day of sunbathing and relaxation by the time you get here. Engineers have yet to tunnel through the west coast cliffs, so the only

Never venture into the mountains without warm clothes – the weather can change in an instant.

way to get to Güigüí is on foot or by boat. Two hikes, from Puerto de la Aldea and Tasartico, reach the beach. Neither is easy, but at two hours, the latter is considerably shorter. A hardy fisherman in Puerto de la Aldea takes groups of up to 20 people to the beach, but it's not cheap, and rough seas often prevent the trip. Be aware that if conditions worsen, he will not be able to collect you, leaving you no alternative but to hike back *(see also p44)*. *Map A4*

10 Puerto de la Aldea

Many say that it is the travelling, not the arriving, that makes the west coast noteworthy, but Puerto de la Aldea is a lovely place to recharge your batteries before continuing along the relentlessly winding roads. For most of the year it's eerily quiet, but you might find a bit of life in the small fishing harbour or one of the excellent seafood restaurants. The small pine wood also warrants a look, as do the pre-Hispanic sites known as Los Caserones. The town becomes more animated on 11 September each year during the Fiesta del Charco, when locals go to the lagoon *(charco)* at the far end of the beach and try to catch fish with their bare hands. *Map A3*

Puerto de la Aldea

Above the Clouds

Morning

This is a full-day drive, so you need to set out no later than 10am. Start off by taking in **Teror**'s important church and museum, before heading for nearby **Valleseco**. The town itself doesn't warrant a stop, but the lush ravines certainly do *(see p84)*. From here, follow the road to Artenara, stopping en route to admire the astounding **Caldera de Los Pinos de Gáldar**. There is little to keep you in Artenara, but the short walk to see the cave-church *(see p82)* is worthwhile. A snaking road from the island's highest town leads you into the dramatic west, passing Acusa *(see p84)* before joining the terrifying GC606 towards Ayacata. A visit to **Roque Nublo** *(see p81)* is a must. The foot of the rock is a superb spot for a picnic lunch, though those who do not fancy the hike may prefer the picnic site further along the road.

Afternoon

After lunch, head up to the island's highest point, Pico de las Nieves *(see p81)*, keeping your fingers crossed for clear skies. A curious museum, the Museo Guayere, located on the GC150, offers an entertaining break from the mountain roads. It is an eccentric collection of old junk crammed into a rather charming cave home. There are decent handicrafts and foodstuffs on sale here, though you might prefer to shop for souvenirs at Cruz de Tejeda. End the day in pretty Tejeda *(see p81)*, enjoying a coffee and one of the local specialities – any of a number of almond biscuits and cakes.

Left **La Cantonera** Right **Cactualdea**

TOP 10 Best of the Rest

1 Mercadillo de San Mateo
Of the numerous *mercadillos* (farmers' markets) held around the island, San Mateo's takes the crown. *C/Antonio Perera Rivero • Map D3 • 8am–8pm Sat, 8am–3pm Sun*

2 La Cantonera, San Mateo
La Cantonera is the island's largest ethnographic museum. Set in a captivating 17th-century house, there are over 12,000 exhibits, including furniture, handicrafts and tools from the town's past. *Avda Tinamar • Map D3 • 10am–4pm Mon–Sat• Adm charge*

3 Caldera de los Marteles
It's not unusual to see livestock grazing at the bottom of this enormous, pine-fringed volcanic crater. It's a good place to stretch your legs and enjoy views of Valsequillo and the capital. *GC130 • Map D3*

4 Ayacata
Villages don't come any prettier than this one, especially in February, when the trees are ablaze with pale pink almond blossom. Stop for a coffee and some delicious marzipan, a local speciality. *Map D3*

5 Andén Verde
"Green Platform" is the rather inapt name given to this bewitching stretch of stark cliffs, which tower above the ocean. Don't miss views from the Mirador del Balcón. *Map B3*

6 Fontanales
The first sight to greet you on your arrival in this friendly *pueblo* is the oversized church. For refreshment, drop in at the Bodega La Parranda, a curious bar with no fixed menu and lots of local character. *Map D2*

7 Acusa
The Acusa flatlands make an odd sight amid the craggy central mountains, and provide a superlative place to get a snap of Roque Nublo *(see p24)*. *Map C3*

8 Cactualdea
The arid west of the island is not known for its plant life, but the climate is ideal for growing cactuses. More than 1,200 species thrive in this private garden. *Carretera del Hoyo • Map B3 • 928 89 12 28 • 10am–6pm daily • Adm charge*

9 La Aldea de San Nicolás Old Quarter
Few travellers venture to Gran Canaria's forgotten town; fewer manage to find its atmospheric old quarter, east of the church *(see also p59)*. *Map B3*

10 Valleseco
The island's most overlooked area is its most charming. Offering little other than its sheer natural beauty, Valleseco is comprised of tiny rural communities connected by roads that fizzle out without warning. The area is known for its quality wooden handicrafts and unparalleled hiking trails. *Map D2*

Avoid the central region after a sprinkling of snow, or you may find yourself trapped in a 3-hour traffic jam.

Las Tirajanas, San Bartolomé de Tirajana

Price Categories

For a three-course meal for one with half a bottle of wine (or equivalent meal), taxes and extra charges.

€	under €20
€€	€20–€30
€€€	€30–€40
€€€€	€40–€50
€€€€€	over €50

Top 10 Places to Eat

1 La Gañanía, La Aldea de San Nicolás

The restaurant serves simple, traditional fare. Its well-kept cactus garden is the ideal place to enjoy a fresh fruit juice. *C/ Albercón 4 • Map B3 • 928 89 01 62 • €€*

2 Restaurante La Oliva, Playa de Tasarte

One of a very few restaurants on the west coast, La Oliva serves first-rate seafood – whatever's fresh on the day. If the tables were any closer to the sea, you'd be in it. *Map A4 • 928 89 43 58 • Lunch only; closed Mon • €*

3 Cueva del Molino, Artenara

Simple home-cooked Canarian cuisine at its best. If you're really hungry, opt for an enormous slab of tender fillet steak. *Avda Matias Vega 23 • Map C3 • 928 66 62 27 • €€€*

4 Paraíso Canario, El Madroñal

A carnivores' paradise. The speciality is steak cooked at your table on a scorching hot rock, but the "sampler" menu, with 300g of meat and five sauces, is also a winner. *Urbanización del Tribunal 8 • Map E3 • 928 64 30 50 • Closed Tue • €€*

5 La Vaguetilla, Vega de San Mateo

Opt for the garden seats with a view of the kids' playground at the elegant, traditional Canarian restaurant. *Avda Tinamar 49 • Map D3 • 928 66 07 64 • Closed Mon • €€*

6 Parador de Cruz de Tejeda, Tejeda

Head up to this hotel restaurant if you're craving elegant dining and magnificent views of the pine forest. The menu features local specialities with a creative twist. *Cruz de Tejeda • Map D3 • 928 01 25 00 • €€€€*

7 Grill El Pesebre, Teror

Meat lovers will go wild for El Pesebre, a vibrant venue for traditional dishes, including enormous platefuls of grilled pork, beef and chicken. Sit inside or on the lovely garden terrace. *C/El Mesón 35 • Map D2 • 928 61 37 46 • Closed Mon • €€€*

8 Las Tirajanas, San Bartolomé de Tirajana

With remarkable views over the Fataga ravine, this is probably the best-located restaurant on the island. *Hotel Las Tirajanas • Map D4 • 928 56 69 69 • €€€*

9 El Refugio, Cruz de Tejeda

Home cooking, local wines and friendly service in a wood-panelled cottage more reminiscent of the Alps than the Canaries. *Cruz de Tejeda • Map D3 • 928 66 65 13 • Open daily until 8pm • €€€*

10 El Prado, Valleseco

In an area noted for its farm produce, you can guarantee the ingredients are fresh. Any of the Canarian stews can be counted on. *C/Alcalde Vicente Arencibia 7 • Map D2 • 928 61 83 07 • Closed Mon, Tue • €€*

For more restaurant listings **See pp60–61, 71, 79, 91 and 99**

Left **Cactuses, Jardín Botánico Viera y Clavijo** Right **Caldera de Bandama**

Eastern Gran Canaria

OFTEN IGNORED, THE EAST OF THE ISLAND *may appear to be something of an industrial wasteland, but away from the featureless motorway lie some of the island's oldest towns, harbouring delightful historical centres. But the area's history doesn't start with the Conquest. This was the most densely populated region in Guanche times, a fact made clear by the varied aboriginal settlements scattered throughout the windswept hill tops and jagged ravines.*

The village of Temisas

Top 10 Sights

1 Jardín Botánico Viera y Clavijo
2 Caldera de Bandama
3 La Atalaya
4 San Francisco, Telde
5 Tufia
6 Telde Beaches
7 Cuatro Puertas
8 Barranco de Guayadeque
9 Agüimes Old Quarter
10 Temisas

1 Jardín Botánico Viera y Clavijo

loriously fresh air and, apart om the sound of birdsong, most total silence provide the erfect escape from the buzz of ie city or the tiring mountain ›ads *(see pp14–15)*.

2 Caldera de Bandama

This striking crater offers fine day trip for hikers, bird- ›atchers, botanists, historians, olfers, and just plain nature ›vers. As an added curiosity, a ardy farmer has opted out of the it race to live in a simple house : the crater's base *(see pp26–7)*.

3 La Atalaya

The best way to see one of ie island's oldest troglodyte ettlements is simply to get lost ı its narrow, winding streets. It difficult to spot the cave homes owadays, as their owners have sually added rather unsightly xtensions. However, if you peek ırough an open door, you'll see ie village's cave origins. Don't ıiss a visit to Ecomuseo Casa anchito, the cave-home and ›orkshop of La Atalaya's most ımous potter *(see p37)*. Next oor is a workshop where local raftsmen produce traditional eramics, which make excellent ouvenirs. *Map E3*

eramics workshop, La Atalaya

4 San Francisco, Telde

If you follow a narrow street opposite the museum, you will find a real jewel, Telde's historical quarter. Some of the island's oldest buildings line the tranquil plazas, hidden away in the labyrinth of cobbled alleys. Look in on the simple Iglesia Conventual de San Francisco, which houses a splendid Baroque stone altarpiece. *Map F3*

Church of San Francisco, Telde

5 Tufia

Intriguingly, no one knows exactly when the Guanche sites were constructed. One thing that can be said of the hilltop settlement at Tufia is that it seems to belong to two different epochs. A group of natural caves just above sea level served as home to primitive dwellers, but the low stone houses crowning the cliff were perhaps the work of a more developed society. Ideally located for spotting unwanted visitors, the village is surrounded by what appears to be a protective wall, suggesting that its people had some knowledge of defensive strategies *(see also pp40–41)*. *Exit 13 from GC1 (El Goro) • Map F3 • Entry by appointment only; • call 928 219 421 ext. 4441 (Cabildo) • Free • No disabled access*

Opt for sturdy footwear when visiting Guanche sites.

Telde beaches

6 Telde Beaches

Telde's town hall has maxi-mized the appeal of the east coast beaches by building a 4-km (3-mile) promenade, creating a lovely coastal walk. Starting in Las Salinetas, summer play-ground of wealthy city dwellers, you progress to Playa de Melenara, a much larger and more characterful beach than its smarter neighbour. There are some excellent fish restaurants here. Then you pass some low, pretty houses and the important harbour at Taliarte; Cofradía de Pescadores is the place to go here for cheap and tasty fish, fresh from the net. Past the lighthouse, the walk briefly leaves the coast to skirt an ugl government building. There then follows a stretch with natural rock pools and rough seas. Playa del Hombre's dangerous waters are favoured by daring surfers; beginners prefe Playa del Hoya del Pozo Playa La Garita is a pleasant strip of black sand lapped by calm seas. The fried octopus served at Casa Santiago is simpl divine. Just behind the beach is a taxi rank, so you need not retrac your steps. *Map F3*

Alternative Energy

Ask any islander what is the worst thing about living in Vecindario and they are likely to offer one response: the wind. Even if you don't venture out of your car, you'll notice it. The palm trees here all lean eastward and women avoid wearing skirts. Windsurfers, of course, are happy with the bracing conditions, along with a group of scientists. Elegant wind turbines are a familiar sight on the eastern landscape, and the Canarian Institute of Technology continues to investigate further applications of wind power.

7 Cuatro Puertas

The main cave takes its nam from its four entrances. Without doubt the most impressive man made caves on the island, the dwellings are connected by sho tunnels, so it is fun to explore. You will also find a rare example of an *almogarén*, a series of sma channels probably used for makir offerings to the gods. *Access from GC100 between Telde and Ingenio • Map F3 • Free • No disabled access*

8 Barranco de Guayadeque

Step back in time in the island's deepest ravine, once heavily populated by Guanches, but now home to just a handful of cave dwellers *(see pp28–9)*.

Barranco de Guayadeque

9 Agüimes Old Quarter

Agüimes was founded in 1487. Already densely populated before the Europeans arrived, it was one of the first post-Conquest settlements. These days, it's hardly a hectic town, as the tourism boom has tempted many inland inhabitants to the coast; but the lack of traffic or modern buildings is precisely what gives Agüimes its charm. A mishmash of traditional and Neo-Classical architecture lines the quiet paved streets, with the crowning glory being the huge Parroquia de San Sebastián *(see p38)*. As well as a top-notch restaurant serving Canarian cuisine *(see p60)*, there is a delightful museum of local history *(see p36)*. *Map E4*

Agüimes old quarter

10 Temisas

A visit to this tiny hamlet is a must for its gorgeous location and charming buildings. This is the best place to admire traditional rural architecture. The nearby olive grove brings income to the village, and Temisas is the island's only producer of olive oil, though it's surprisingly difficult to find anywhere to buy it here. *GC550 Map E4*

A Day in the East

Morning

Once passengers have sampled **Santa Brígida**'s wines *(see p90)*, head to **La Atalaya** *(see p87)* to buy some traditional ceramics. Then make the round trip to the awesome **Caldera de Bandama** *(see pp26–7)*, allowing at least an hour if you intend to explore on foot. Take the GC80 to **Telde** *(see p87)*, and wander around the old town, which is also a good place to stop for a coffee. You can delve into the region's history at the **Cuatro Puertas caves** on the GC100. Carry on to **Ingenio**, stopping at the Museo de Piedras to buy local crafts. The town centre here is worth a look, but a better option for lunch is the **Barranco de Guayadeque** *(see pp28–9)*, with its cave restaurants and scenic picnic sites. Allow an hour to drive along the ravine.

Afternoon

The next stop is **Agüimes**, with its cathedral-like church and interesting history museum. From here, it is a rather winding drive to **Temisas**, a pretty village overlooking the Barranco del Polvo. After soaking up the atmosphere of one of the island's last traditional hamlets, you can either backtrack past Agüimes and onto the GC1, or continue past **La Sorrueda**, taking the GC65 to meet the main motorway. Whizz north to **Playa de Salinetas**, leave your car, and enjoy an easy walk along the coast. The beachside bars at Playa de Melenara are good for a coffee or a beer before you continue your stroll to Playa de la Garita.

Agüimes is famed for its bread – stock up when you visit it.

Left **Basílica de San Juan Bautista, Telde** Right **Juan Grande**

TOP 10 Best of the Rest

1 Golf

Spain's first golf club was originally located in Las Palmas, but later moved to a new site at a more prestigious location, in Bandama. Nearby is another fine course, El Cortijo, host to international competitions. Both are open to non-members on week-day mornings. *Real Club de Golf de Las Palmas: Ctra de Bandama s/n, Sta Brígida. Map E3. 928 35 01 04. www.realclubdegolfdelaspalmas.com • El Cortijo Golf Center: Autovía del Sur, km 6.4, Telde. Map F3. 928 684 890.*

2 Basílica de San Juan Bautista, Telde

Begun in 1519, this is one of the oldest churches on the island. It took five centuries to reach its present form; the Neo-Gothic towers were added early last century *(see also p38)*. *Plaza de San Juan • Map F3 • 928 69 02 85 • Open 9am–12:30pm, 5–8pm daily • Free*

3 Casa-Museo León y Castillo, Telde

Politician Fernando de León y Castillo and his engineer brother Juan grew up in this lovely house, of interest for its perfect *mudéjar* architecture. *C/León y Castillo 43–45 • Map F3 • 928 69 13 77 • 9am– 8pm Mon–Fri, 10am–8pm Sat, 10am–1pm Sun • Free • www.fernandoleonycastillo.com*

4 Valsequillo Villages

Valsequillo itself has little to hold you for more than a few minutes, but the surrounding villages ooze character. *Map E3*

5 Ingenio Old Quarter

Penetrate Ingenio's ugly urban sprawl and you will find its peaceful historic centre. The town is known for its crafts. *Map E4*

6 Wine Tasting in Santa Brígida

Find a teetotaller to drive you around the island's wine district. Most *bodegas* don't hold official tasting sessions, but will let you try before you buy. *Map E3*

7 Letreros de Balos

The cave drawings in the Balos ravine are considered the most important in the islands. Human figures, geometric shapes and zoomorphic forms have been painstakingly etched over a huge area of basaltic rock. *Dirt track off GC104 between Cruce de Arinaga and Corralillos • Map E4 • 928 21 94 21 ext 4441 • Visits by appointment only • Free*

8 Arinaga

Although skirted by an unlovely industrial estate, this small fishing village has enough charm to warrant a visit. *Map F*

9 Pozo Izquierdo

Windsurfers from across the globe congregate here in summer for the championships, and many stay year-round. *Map E5*

10 Juan Grande

Fans of historic buildings will enjoy a brief visit to Juan Grande, home to a once ramshackle mansion and church. *Map E5*

Satautey, Monte Lentiscal

Price Categories

For a three-course meal for one with half a bottle of wine (or equivalent meal), taxes and extra charges.

€	under €20
€€	€20–€30
€€€	€30–€40
€€€€	€40–€50
€€€€€	over €50

10 Places to Eat

1 El Oroval, Agüimes

The restaurant of the rural hotel Casa de los Camellos serves a range of creative Canarian dishes. The tasting menu is recommended. *C/El Progreso 12 • Map E4 • 928 78 50 03 • €€€*

2 Nelson, Arinaga

The area's most noted fish restaurant is equally well known for its extensive wine list. Magnificent ocean views accompany the catch of the day. *Avda Polizón 7, Playa de Arinaga • Map F5 • 928 18 08 0 • Closed Sun • €€€€€*

3 Cinco Jotas, Telde

If you haven't sampled *jamón Serrano*, this smart restaurant overlooking the El Cortijo golf course is the place to do so – the *tapas* menu offers a dozen varieties. *El Cortijo golf course (see opposite) • Map F3 • 928 69 5 20 • Closed Sun L • €€*

4 Bar Restaurante Monzón, Valsequillo

Small in size, but big on flavour, this family restaurant packs a punch with its home cooking delivered with extra care. *Plaza San Miguel 3 • Map E3 • 928 70 0 43 • €*

5 Señorio de Agüimes, Agüimes

Excellent Canarian cuisine served in an enchanting early-1900s building. *C/Juan Ramón Jiménez • Map E4 • 928 78 97 66 • Closed Sun D • €€*

6 Satautey, Monte Lentiscal

Appetizers and desserts stand out at the Hotel Escuelas smart dining room. The Canarian combination starter is a great way to try a mouthful of the island's most typical dishes. *C/Real de Coello 2 • Map E2 • 828 01 04 21 • €€€*

7 Jardín Canario, Tafira

Not only do you get delicious traditional cuisine, you also get a lovely garden view at this elegant restaurant. Grab a table on the terrace. *Ctra del Centro km 7 • Map E2 • 928 35 52 45 • €€€*

8 Bodegón Vandama, Bandama

A simply marvellous location to dine – in a stupendous traditional building with views of the crater *(see pp26–7)*. The house red is fermented in the adjoining winery. *Ctra Bandama 116 • Map E3 • 928 35 27 54 • Closed Mon, Tue, Sun D • €€*

9 Las Grutas de Artiles, Las Meleguinas, nr Sta Brígida

The dining areas in this cave-restaurant are connected by tunnels. Canarian classics like *potaje de berros (see p61)* are served along with some superb cuts of meat. *C/Las Meleguinas • Map E3 • 928 64 05 75 • Closed Tue • €€€*

10 Restaurante El Guajara, Valsequillo

A simple, family-run place specializing in excellent meat grills. *Las Vegas de Valsequillo • Map E3 • 928 70 54 79 • Closed Mon • €€*

For more restaurant listings **See pp60–61, 71, 79, 85 and 99**

Left **Palmitos Park** Right **Fataga**

Southern Gran Canaria

IF THE NORTH OF GRAN CANARIA IS CHARACTERIZED *by its lush green gullies, then shades of brown and yellow are the colours of the south. For centuries, the arid coast was virtually uninhabited, until holidaymakers discovered its perfect climate and fine golden beaches. Inland, the dry plains give way to wide ravines before pine forests begin to appear. Though the area lacks the rich heritage of other parts of the island, it more than makes up for this with sun, sand, family days out and wild nightlife.*

Presa de las Niñas

Sights

1. **Maspalomas**
2. **Mundo Aborigen**
3. **Arteara**
4. **Palmitos Park**
5. **Pilancones**
6. **Fataga**
7. **La Fortaleza de Ansite**
8. **Las Presas**
9. **Villages in Mogán**
10. **Puerto de Mogán**

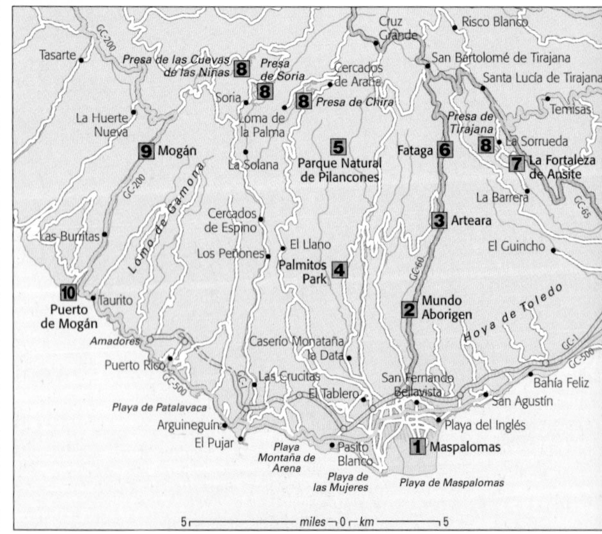

1 Maspalomas

The extensive sand dunes and palm-fringed lagoon set this tourist resort apart from the rest *(see pp18–19)*.

2 Mundo Aborigen

Anyone intrigued by the enigmatic pre-Hispanic culture of the island would do well to visit Mundo Aborigen. This open-air museum brings Guanche culture to life with scale models of homes, tombs, meeting places and sacred sites. The buildings are peopled with life-size models of the early inhabitants. There are over 100 Guanche models, some of them rather graphic, such as one of a poor wretch having his skull punctured on a visit to the doctor. *GC60 • Map D5 • 928 172 295 • 9am–6pm daily • Adm charge*

Maspalomas dunes

3 Arteara

Although the graves have long since been looted, this cemetery remains an important stop on a tour of the island's sites of archeological interest. Making out the circular tombs among the debris of a stark lava field is not easy, but information panels help you to differentiate the sepulchres from the other rocks. The site covers an area 2 km (1 mile) wide and was once encircled by a low stone wall, remnants of which can still be seen dotted about. *GC60 • Map D5 • Free • No disabled access*

4 Palmitos Park

Even the staunchest zoo-haters agree that the animals here look healthy. Originally a tropical-bird sanctuary, the park has widened its remit to include primates and reptiles, as well as a few small mammals. The lush location heightens the impression of a tropical paradise, no doubt contributing to the animals' cheerful disposition. If flora appeals more than fauna, you will enjoy the excellent botanical gardens, featuring both endemic and exotic plants and lauded by naturalists. The small but comprehensive orchid house is a delight *(see also pp52–3)*. *Access via GC503 • Map C5 • 928 797 070 • www.palmitospark.es • 10am–6pm daily • Adm charge*

5 Pilancones

Approached from the barren south, the sudden appearance of this verdant pine forest is a shock. The view from the GC65 is impressive, but for a closer look, leave your car at Cruz Grande and hike into its depths. Several devastating forest fires have left the area charred in places, creating a somewhat ghostly atmosphere. Only the distant tapping of the great spotted woodpecker disturbs the silence in this little-visited wilderness. *Map C4*

Mundo Aborigen

Summer temperatures here can be excruciating, so have plenty of water and suncream with you, even if you're just driving.

Quality versus Quantity

More and more tourists visit the island each year, but the amount of money going to local entrepreneurs is slight, thanks to the rise of the all-inclusive holiday. The *cabildo* (council) is now trying to promote quality tourism alongside the bums-on-seats approach. Upmarket resorts such as Maspalomas, Meloneras and Puerto de Mogán are slowly changing the island's image, while rural tourism is also taking off.

6 Fataga

Fataga manages to retain its charm despite the ever-growing number of visitors keen to admire its bucolic architecture. The cluster of restaurants on the main road still offer good Canarian cuisine, and there is a bodega, which sells the only wine produced in the south. After visiting the small church, wander the labyrinth of cobbled passageways and look out over the ravine that shares the village's name. *Map F4*

7 La Fortaleza de Ansite

This immense natural fort is one of the island's most notable pre-Hispanic sites, and is certainly worthy of having hosted the last stand of the Guanches. An arresting tunnel, 34 m (112 ft) long and 18 m (60 ft) wide, cuts through the massive rock, while numerous caves, both natural and man-made, are dotted about. When victory eluded the natives, many of them hurled themselves into the surrounding ravines, favouring death to slavery. The end of the Conquest was celebrated on 29 April 1485, when the remaining Guanches were frog-marched into the capital to concede defeat. *GC651 • Map D4 • Free • No disabled access*

8 Las Presas

With limited rainfall and highly porous soil, water conservation is a crucial factor in Canarian life, so it's little surprise that the southern *presas* (reservoirs) are important meeting-places for the islanders. They attract hikers, picnickers, fishermen and even bathers, though the latter activity is not strictly allowed. The south's biggest *presa* is Soria, the most remote is Chira, and the title of most beautiful is a toss-up between the pine-flanked Presa de las Niñas *(see pp42–3)* and the palm-lined oasis at La Sorrueda. *Soria: Map C4 • Chira: Map C4 • Presa de las Niñas: Map C4 • La Sorrueda: Map D4*

La Fortaleza de Ansite

lolino de Viento, a village near Mogán

9 Villages in Mogán

The rural lifestyle found in ther parts of the island is hard o spot in the south, where the armers have long since moved o the coast in search of tourism-ased jobs; but it's still possible o sample traditional life near Mogán. Rustic architecture revails here, particularly in the Moorish village of Veneguera nd in the many hamlets south f Mogán itself. Step back in me in Molino de Viento, where etired farmers congregate under ne restored windmill to discuss fe before mass tourism. *Map B4*

10 Puerto de Mogán

Although on the endangered st, pretty Puerto de Mogán as so far managed to avoid ne building frenzy that plagues ther areas of the south coast. he authorities here have opted o lodge tourists in a low-rise omplex that houses fewer isitors, but is certainly easier n the eye than the towering 960s hotels favoured elsewhere. he quiet harbour is a fabulous lace to eat seafood and then while away an afternoon on a oat trip. Try to arrive early, efore the tourist buses break ne silence and the small beach lls up with bathers. *Map B5*

Family Fun

Morning

Leave your car, if you have one, in Arguineguin, and catch the bus to **Puerto de Mogán**. Arrive early, and enjoy the peace and quiet of the island's most charming resort, before jumping on a glass-bottomed boat back to **Arguineguin**, a two-hour trip. On the way you will pass steep cliffs and secluded beaches before reaching the rather over-built resort of Puerto Rico, where you have to change boats. Arguineguin is a lovely fishing town, so far immune to the mass tourism closing in on all sides. The ultra-calm waters are ideal for children, and plenty of restaurants offer kids' menus. Los Pescaítos, at the western end of the promenade, is near the natural pools. Apolo 11, on the main road, has more local character, but fewer dishes for young ones.

Afternoon

After lunch, whizz along the motorway to **Maspalomas** *(see pp18–19)*. Not far from the lighthouse, there is a "camel station"; a short ride on a dromedary is the perfect way to enjoy the splendid dunes. Allow time for the magnificent beach, then hit the road again, this time heading north.

Mundo Aborigen *(see p95)* offers an educational yet entertaining insight into Canarian history – helpful before visiting **Arteara** *(see p95)*. You'll need half an hour to scramble over the rocks at this Guanche cemetery. Continue north to **Fataga**, where frazzled parents may appreciate the *bodega* hidden away among the pretty alleyways.

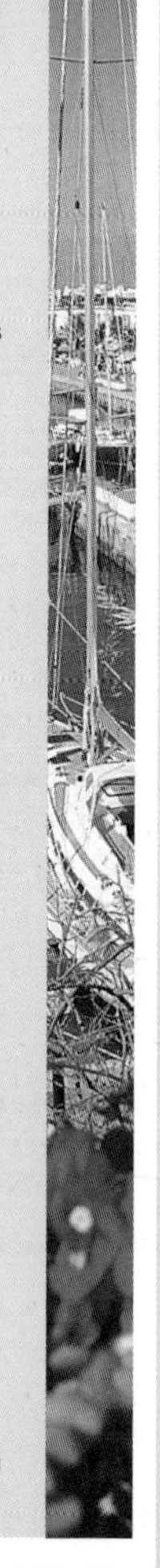

Don't miss Mogán's romería (see p55), *a traditional party held in June.*

Left **Drag show, Ricky's Bar, Yumbo Centrum** Right **Aqua Ocean Club, Meloneras**

TOP 10 Nightspots

1 Yumbo Centrum, Playa del Inglés

The Yumbo Centre – by day a regular shopping mall, by night a heaving mass of drag queens and leather-clad party-goers – is the epicentre of the island's gay nightlife scene. Size up the bars before you head in; some have firm dress codes or are strictly men only. Ricky's Cabaret Bar is a fun, welcoming place. *Avda de Estados Unidos 54 • Map D6*

2 Casino Tamarindos, San Agustín

If thumping dance music and cringe-making karaoke are not for you, the casino may be your best bet for a night out. As well as the usual games, there's a nightly cabaret and a decent restaurant. *C/Las Retamas 3 • Map D6*

3 Chinawhite, Playa del Inglés

The minimalist decor and banging beats attract a young and fashion-able set to this funky bar. *CC Kasbah, Avda de Tenerife • Map D6*

4 Joker Disco, Puerto Rico

Top international DJs and stylish surroundings have earned Joker Disco a reputation as one of the best clubs in Puerto Rico. There are plenty of lively party nights. *Centro Comercial • Map B5*

5 Pacha, Playa del Inglés

The big boys of the club world rock the southern coastline with this multi-lounge disco, drawing dance crowds from all over the island. *Avda Alferez Provisionales s/n • Map D6*

6 Heaven, Playa del Inglés

All are welcome at this class branch of Europe's top gay club, favoured by big groups of wome on hen nights. *Yumbo Centrum, Avda de Estados Unidos • Map D6*

7 Disco My Song, Maspalomas

If you feel that Latin fever, head over to Disco My Song in Holida World on a Thursday, Friday or Saturday night. Some of Spain's best Latino performers play here *Avda Touroperador Tui • Map D6*

8 Garage, Playa del Inglés

Cheap and cheerful, this slightly run-down bar at the edg of the Kasbah is a good place to start the night. *CC Kasbah, Avda de Tenerife • Map D6*

9 Bachira, Playa del Inglés

One of the resort's most stylish nightspots is also its busiest, packed to the gills with revellers until 6 or 7am. Local DJs play European dance music. *Avd de Italia (opposite CC Kasbah) • Map D6*

10 Aqua Ocean Club, Meloneras

This sprawling nightclub in front of the Hotel H10 Playa Melonera Palace attracts a huge crowd to its disco, ambient terrace and three bars. *Centro Comercial, Play Meloneras • Map D6*

Price Categories

For a three-course meal for one with half a bottle of wine (or equivalent meal), taxes and extra charges.	
€	under €20
€€	€20–€30
€€€	€30–€40
€€€€	€40–€50
€€€€€	over €50

amira, Playa del Aguila

10 Places to Eat

1 El Portalón, Playa del Inglés
Jose Cruz López prepares nouthwatering cuisine from his ative Basque country. *Hotel ;ol Barbacán, Avda Tirajana 27 • Map D6 928 77 20 30 • €€€*

2 Ristorante Rimini, Playa del Inglés
Rimini is a reminder that there's nore to Italian food than pizza and asta. The venison *flambé* and veal teak stand out, and there's plenty or vegetarians. *Avda Tenerife 11 Map D6 • 928 76 43 64 • €€€€*

3 Bamira, Playa del Aguila
Cutting-edge cuisine at the estaurant that introduced fusion ood to the Canaries. Try the pinach-and-garlic mousse or the ather unusual beetroot sorbet. *C/Los Pinos 11 • Map D6 • 928 76 76 6 • Closed Wed • €€€€*

4 Q Tal, Puerto de Mogán
A funky, chilled-out joint with ıst a few choices cooked to order. Book ahead if you want to sample he evening menu – a 7-course east of creative gourmet cuisine. *Between main harbour and fishing arbour • Map B5 • 928 56 55 34 • Closed Sun • €€ (lunch), €€€€€ (dinner)*

5 Los Guayres, Puerto de Mogán
Canarian classics meet gourmet uisine at this excellent restaurant. There's even a separate dessert oom. *Hotel Cordial Mogán Playa, vda de Canarias s/n • Map B5 • 928 72 1 00 • Closed Sun, Mon • €€€€€*

6 Bali Meloneras, Meloneras
If you're looking for something a little different, head for some oriental spice at this high-class Indonesian restaurant. Reservations recommended. *C/ Mar Mediterráneo 2 • Map D6 • 928 14 33 75 • €€€€*

7 La Casa Vieja, Maspalomas
For a taste of true Canarian cuisine, you could do a lot worse than the rustic Casa Vieja. It's the authentic experience, with local food, local musicians and traditional decor. *Ctra A. Fataga 139 • Map D6 • 928 76 90 10 • €€€*

8 Anno Domini, San Agustín
An upmarket restaurant in a rather unprepossessing shopping centre. Chef Jacques Truyol gives a personal touch to some favourite French dishes, adding a Canarian flavour here and there. *CC San Agustín • Map D6 • 928 76 29 15 • €€€*

9 Samsara, Maspalomas
For a chilled-out dining experience, this oriental restaurant offers comfortable terrace sofas and an art gallery. *Avda del Oasis 30 • Map D6 • 928 14 27 36 • Closed Mon • €€€*

10 La Aquarela, Patalavaca
This elegant poolside restaurant was one of the first on the island to offer *nouvelle cuisine*. The duck and sautéed prawns are highly recommended. *Apartamentos Aguamarina • Map C6 • 928 73 58 91 • Closed Mon • €€€*

For more restaurant listings **See pp60–61, 71, 79, 85 and 91**

STREETSMART

Left **Official tourist information kiosk** Right **www.spain-grancanaria.com website**

Top 10 Planning Your Trip

1 When to Visit

The Canary Islands' climate is mild year-round. Prices double over Christmas and Easter. August and July are busy and can be sweltering. May, June and October are quieter and less hot; for most, these are the ideal months to visit. Rains drape a cloak of green over the mountains in January and February.

2 What to Bring

You'll be able to buy almost anything you need in Gran Canaria, but it's a good idea to pack ample supplies of any medication you are taking, or at least make a note of the active ingredients, as Spanish brand names are often different. Buy toiletries and beachwear on arrival.

3 What Type of Trip?

What you want from your holiday will dictate when you visit and where you stay. Hikers and nature-lovers will prefer the winter months in the mountains; sun-worshippers, May–October on the south coast.

4 Passports and Visas

The general requirement for entry into Spain is a passport valid for 90 days beyond the end of your stay. EU citizens from countries within the Schengen Agreement can carry a valid ID card in lieu of a passport. A visa is not required for citizens of EU member states. Americans, Canadians, Australians and New Zealanders can stay with no visa for up to 90 days.

5 Customs

Although part of Spain, the Canary Islands are not classed as being within the EU for customs purposes, and the limits are strict. Where duty-free is concerned, you can bring in or take out 1 litre of spirits, 2 litres of wine, 200 cigarettes and 60 ml of perfume. If returning to another EU country, you must use the red or green customs channels rather than the blue one.

6 Electricity and Water

The standard two-pin European plug is used. The electricity supply is 220 V, 50 Hz; visitors from the USA will need to purchase a converter, as well as an adaptor, in advance. Tap water is not recommended for drinking, though it is fine for brushing your teeth.

7 Time

The islands observe GMT and BST, so mainland Spain is always an hour ahead. When it is noon in Gran Canaria, it is 7am in New York and 4am in Los Angeles.

8 Language

The local version of Spanish has a few curiosities, but none that will cause problems if you can speak *castellano*. Most Canarians are more than keen to practise their English-language skills.

9 Online Planning

The tourist board has an excellent website with lots of information and links. Another good source is www.spain-grancanaria.com, offering up-to-date information on weather, events, car hire and accommodation.

www.grancanaria.com

10 Local Tourist Information Offices

Virtually every reasonably-sized town has a tourist office, usually open weekday mornings only.

Consulates in Las Palmas

France
928 20 23 71

Germany
928 49 18 80

Ireland
928 29 77 28

Italy
928 24 19 11

Netherlands
928 36 22 51

Sweden
928 26 17 51

Switzerland
928 15 79 79

United Kingdom
902 10 93 56

USA
928 27 12 59

Preceding pages **Outdoor tables at a café in the Triana district of Las Palmas**

ɘft **Flight departing from Gran Canaria Airport** Right **Inter-island ferry**

10 Getting to and Around Gran Canaria

1 Charter Flights from Europe

lost holidaymakers get) the island on charter ghts. It takes about four ours to fly from London) Gran Canaria Airport, 3 km (14 miles) south f the capital. If a meal is ot included, think about acking your own, as in- ght food can be pricey. *Thomas Cook Airlines: ww.flythomascook.com Thomson Airways: www. omsonflights.co.uk*

2 By Air from Mainland Spain

S visitors will have to ass through an airport on e mainland – almost ertainly either Madrid or arcelona. Onward flights) Gran Canaria take a tle over two hours. ✆ *ueling: www.vueling.com*

3 By Ferry from Mainland Spain

ardcore boat fans, those ho loathe flying, and ose wishing to bring eir own cars are about e only travellers who opt r the arduous ferry ossing from Cadiz. The urney, operated by cciona Trasmediterranea, kes two days on seas at can be far from calm.

4 Cruises

As the capital has uch an important port, it a major stopoff point r cruise ships. Unfortu ately, their passengers o not have the time to et much further than e city centre.

5 Package Deals

Most visitors to the island opt for a cheap, hassle-free package deal including flights, transfers and accommodation.

6 Getting There from the Other Islands

Two airlines and three maritime companies provide excellent links between Gran Canaria and the six other Canary Islands. There are particularly good connections to Tenerife, which can be reached by boat in a little over an hour. Planes are quicker, but considerably more expensive.
✆ *Inter-island flights: Binter Canarias, www.binter canaries.com; Canaryfly, www.canaryfly.es • Inter-island ferries: Fred Olsen, www.fredolsen.es; Acciona Trasmediterránea, www. trasmediterranea.es; Naviera Armas, www. navieraarmas.com.*

7 Getting Around by Car

Driving is by far the easiest way to see the island and there are plenty of companies offering car hire. You must be over 21 and need to show your driving licence, passport and a credit card. It is a good idea to nominate more than one authorized driver, as the winding roads can be tiring to drive. Speed limits are 120 kph (75 mph) on motorways and 50 kph (30 mph) in built-up areas, unless otherwise signed. ✆ *Autos Vélez: 928 27 71 30 • Autos Moreno: 928 27 71 42, • Cicar: 928 76 76 54, www.cicar.com*

8 Getting Around by Bus

City buses are efficient and quite cheap, especially if you buy a multi-journey ticket *(see p107)*. Route coverage is comprehensive. The *guaguas* that navigate the island are also good, reaching even tiny *pueblos*. The only downside is that services may be infrequent, and you often need to return to a busy town for connections to remoter areas. ✆ *Global: 902 93 94 07, www.globalsu.net*

9 Cycling

Many companies in the capital and the south offer bicycle hire. Cycling is fine within the resorts, but not much fun in congested Las Palmas. You will need to be in shape to cross the island on two wheels, though it is certainly a fantastic way to see the countryside.

10 On Foot

The island is a hiker's dream, with a good network of paths, though signposting might not always be up to date. Paths often include long stretches with no shade, so plenty of water, sunscreen and a decent hat are all vital.

Discounts on inter-island transport are available to the under-25s.

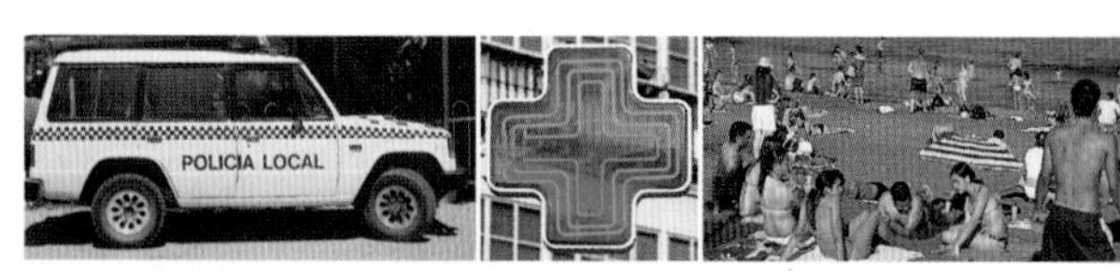

Left **Four-wheel-drive police car** Middle **Pharmacy sign** Right **Sunbathers**

Top 10 Security and Health

1 Insurance

It is always a good idea to take out travel insurance to cover you for private health care, theft and cancellations. Although citizens of the EU are entitled to medical attention with an EHIC *(see below)*, it is more convenient to have private cover. You can then visit any nearby clinic. Private treatment has to be paid for up front, so keep any receipts to send to the insurer on your return.

2 EHIC

Citizens of EU countries are entitled to the same state health care as residents on production of an EHIC (European Health Insurance Card), obtained before leaving home. Payment may be required for some treatments.

3 Clinics and Hospitals

In an emergency, head for the *urgencias* section of either of the large hospitals in Las Palmas: Hospital Doctor Negrín and Hospital Insular. For non-urgent cases, there are clinics in every town. Generally, a *clínica* is private, while a *centro de salud* or *ambulatorio* is run by the state. Ask in your hotel or at a tourist information point for an English- or German-speaking doctor; there are scores in the southern resorts, though they do not come cheap.

4 Emergencies

In an emergency, call 112. English-speaking operators will connect you. There are also free direct numbers for the police and fire brigade *(see directory box below)*.

5 Lost Passports

Report the loss or theft of your passport to the police and get a stamped copy of the statement. Take this to your consulate as soon as possible. Dealing with a situation of this kind is easier – and quicker – if you have two copies of all your documents, one with you and one left with a trusted individual at home.

6 Motion Sickness

The mountainous interior is the bane of those who suffer from travel sickness. Apart from taking medication, the best advice is to eat a light meal before you set off, get plenty of fresh air, and keep your eyes on a fixed point ahead of you.

7 Sunburn

Although the climate may seem mild, the sun is potent. Avoid the hottest part of the day, from noon until 3pm, and reapply sunscreen frequently, even if it seems cloudy.

8 Pharmacies

Every town has at least one *farmácia*, where you can get basic medical advice as well as over-the-counter and prescription medicines. The usual opening hours are 9am–1:30pm and 4–8pm Monday to Friday. Check pharmacy windows to locate your nearest out-of-hours service.

9 Police

The three branches of the Spanish police are the Guardia Civil, the Policía Nacional and the Policía Local. They have different responsibilities, but don't worry about which to turn to in an emergency. The police are generally helpful and will point you in the right direction if they cannot assist you themselves.

10 Crime

Serious crime is rare even in Las Palmas, provided you stay away from certain zones *(see p106)*. Look after your bags and wallets in markets and on busy beaches, but don't be unduly concerned, as even minor crimes are an infrequent occurence.

Useful phone numbers

Emergency: *112*

Fire Service: *080*

Guardia Civil: *062*

Policía Local: *092*

Policía Nacional: *091*

Red Cross: *928 222 222*

Coast Guard: *062*

eft **Postbox** Middle **Public telephone** Right **ATM**

10 Banking and Communications

1 Currency

Locals say life has ecome more expensive ince the euro arrived in 002, but the islands are till cheaper than many uropean countries. Euro anknotes have seven enominations: 500, 200, 00, 50, 20, 10 and 5. here are eight coins: 2 nd 1 euros, and 50, 20, 0, 5, 2 and 1 cents.

2 Changing Money

You can change noney at banks, casas e *cambio* and hotels. The ormer generally offer the est rate, while the latter hould be reserved for bsolute emergencies. hop around for a good ate and make sure that ommission is included.

3 ATMs

You will find at least ne ATM in all but the iniest of towns, and this s the best way to get uros, often giving a etter exchange rate han a bank or *bureau de hange*. Work out how nuch you will need for a ew days so as not to pay epeated commissions.

4 Travellers' Cheques

ravellers' Cheques can e changed at banks and *ureaux de change*, and y and large at a better ate than cash. Opt for a vell-known brand, such s Thomas Cook, Barclays r American Express, and y to get euro cheques o cut down on charges. Remember to take your passport and a note of where you are staying.

5 Money Transfers

As a real last resort you can have money wired to you instantly through Western Union. Most reasonably-sized post offices offer this service, but it is costly, with the sender being charged a commission of around 10 per cent.

6 Locutorios

Perhaps the most convenient place to call home from is a *locutorio*, a small shop offering special rates for overseas calls. They might not be dirt cheap, but it is certainly more economical than calling from a phone box. They also sell phone cards *(see below)*.

7 Telephone Cards

If you plan to phone home more than once, it is worth buying a card. Consult the price lists on display in newsagents and *locutorios*, and choose the card offering the best rates to your country. Most have two separate tariffs, depending on whether you call from a free number or pay a local call rate as well.

8 Post

Post offices in small towns usually open only in the morning, though larger branches in Las Palmas and Playa del Inglés stay open until 2pm. Newsagents and souvenir shops also sell stamps.

9 Internet

Internet cafés are known as *cibers* and are abundant in certain areas, such as Las Palmas and the southern resorts. You may struggle to find one in the smaller towns. A good rate is €1.00 per hour, and you certainly should not pay any more than twice that. In most *cibers* you pay in advance at a desk, though some have convenient coin-operated computers.

10 Press and Broadcasting

There are two local Spanish-language news-papers, *Canarias 7* and *La Provincia*; both are good places to find out about concerts and other events. The informative regional TV channel is, of course, in Spanish. Try Tenerife-based paper *Island Connections* for local news in English. *Info Canarias* keeps German tourists up to date. The foreign press is widely available in the tourist resorts, and a few kiosks in Las Palmas also sell both the local papers and international editions of Europe's leading dailies. Between San Agustín and Puerto de Mogán there are several foreign-language radio stations, and most large hotels have satellite television.

Left **Rally roads** Right **Hiking sign**

Top 10 Things to Avoid

1 Timeshare Touts

The only way to avoid these pests completely is to steer clear of the tourist resorts. Sometimes you can make it work to your advantage, if they're offering free tickets to an attraction you want to visit, but given the amount of time you have to spend listening to their *spiel*, it generally isn't worth it.

2 The Midday Sun

More than a few holidaymakers are fooled by the seemingly cool or cloudy weather, and end up getting terribly sunburnt. Follow the locals' lead and head indoors for a long lunch or a *siesta*, avoiding the hottest part of the day.

3 Angry Drivers

Take care as a pedestrian in Las Palmas. Most local drivers don't like stopping at zebra crossings, and many seem to think that an amber traffic light means speed up. Even if you have a green light, check twice before stepping into the road.

4 Tap Water

Although it won't actually harm you, the island's tap water has a particularly high chlorine content and could not be described as pleasant. It's best to stick to one of the numerous brands of cheap mineral water, many bottled locally.

5 Being Caught Out by the Weather

Fooled by the island's reputation as a sunny paradise, many tourists venture rashly into the mountains in shorts and sandals, only to discover wind, rain and sometimes even snow. Be aware that the climate changes considerably as you move around the island, and always have a jumper handy.

6 Rally Roads

Few visitors who have travelled the island by car leave without feeling a degree of frustration with the endless bends in the roads. Alas, if you really want to explore Gran Canaria, the winding roads are a necessary evil. Try alternating a day of mountain driving with a day spent by the coast or exploring towns on foot. And don't make your itinerary too punishing – there are lots of wonderful lookout points where you can break up your journey.

7 Guided Tours

There are some excellent companies offering guided tours of the island, but do your homework before signing up. The less scrupulous ones will whizz through the top sights in order to give you time to spend your hard-earned euros in some designated shop where the organizers get a high commission.

8 Restaurant and Bar Touts

These unwelcome PR operatives aren't out to con you, but their constant invitations to restaurants, cafés and bars can become extremely wearing. Sadly, the touts just won't be ignored, and sometimes the best option can be to try to strike up a deal – free drinks, for instance. You'l either get a bargain or they'll leave you alone.

9 Incorrect Hiking Information

Before setting off on a hike, you should contact the tourist information office for up-to-date maps and advice. It's also a good idea to ask in the nearest town or village to make sure that the route still exists and is safe. Some of the walking information is dangerously out of date, and heavy rainfall can turn even the best-kept path into a death trap.

10 Las Palmas's Sleazy Zones

Steer clear of Calle Molinos de Viento, near Calle León y Castillo, in the central part of the city – it's a hangout for drug-pushers, prostitutes and pimps. The grotty hotels and sex shops around Calle Tomás Mille and Parque Santa Catalina are likewise a magnet for some rather unsavoury characters.

.eft **Festival del Pino, Teror** Middle **Picnics** Right **Bono de guagua (bus tickets)**

10 Budget Tips

1 Camping

If you don't mind iving without home :omforts, you can save lot of money by using :amp sites. The *cabildo* ias over a dozen free :amp sites across the sland, although most ave no amenities at all. 'here are a few private ;ites charging a minimal ee and offering decent acilities like hot showers nd a bar. Be aware that :amping in an undesig-nated site is illegal.

2 Visit in Low Season

'rices rise sharply in high eason – December, :hristmas, Carnival, Easter and the summer ;chool holidays. You'll nake a reasonable saving y avoiding these times.

3 Menu del Día

Eating out is a costly ffair. The three-course et menu is a superb way o save money. Most estaurants offer the deal t lunchtime only, charging etween €6 and €9 for a neal including one drink water, wine or beer) and ither coffee or dessert, ut the price will start to ise if you start ordering xtra beverages.

4 Bus Passes

Buy a *bono de guagua* s soon as you arrive in .as Palmas. It's a bus icket worth 10 journeys vithin the city, offering lmost a 50 per cent iscount on fares. There's a similar ticket for use on the island–wide buses, called a *tarjeta insular*. The former is available at most newsagents, while the latter is only on sale at large bus stations.

5 Festivals

Thanks to the excellent climate, the island hosts plenty of open-air festivals. In the summer months there's almost always a small concert or show being staged somewhere, usually free. Some of the island's biggest events are gratis, such as Carnival and any of the exciting local street parties *(romerías)*.

6 Budget Accommodation

Albergues are the cheap-est option, but most of them only accept tourists in large groups, of more than 15. In towns, look out for signs proclaiming *hostal* or *pensión*. Both offer cheap lodgings, usually in basic rooms with no TV or air con-ditioning, and often with shared bathrooms.

7 Picnics

The weather and landscape offer perfect conditions for picnicking, and there's no lack of organized picnic spots, though of course you can stop for lunch wherever you want to. Visit one of the farmers' markets early in the day to stock up on fresh fruit and excellent home-made bread and cheese.

8 Long Term and Large Numbers

Many apartments and budget hotels offer reductions if you stay for a minimum of four or five days. Likewise, car hire gets cheaper the longer you keep the car. Some museums and other attractions offer discounts for groups of more than 10 people, so it can make sense to club together with other cost-conscious travellers.

9 Last-minute Bargains

If you can wait until the last minute, you can often pick up a good bargain, especially if you don't mind not knowing where you'll be staying. Some tour operators offer a "mystery holiday", in which you only find out the name of your hotel once you have arrived on the island. There are also some excellent late flight deals for those who prefer to find their own lodgings.

10 Free Attractions

Experiencing Gran Canaria without spending too much money isn't difficult. Some of the best museums are free to enter, as are all of the Guanche sites, nature spots, beaches and *miradors*. In fact, it can be easier to save money than to spend it!

If you're camping, it's best to bring as many supplies as possible from home. For important Canarian camping regulations **See p108**

Left **Camping** Right **A hostel**

Top 10 Accommodation Tips

1 Rural Tourism
Just because the island is famous for its beaches, it doesn't mean you have to stay on the coast. Further inland, there are some wonderful rural hotels and self-catering cottages, providing a perfect base for hikers and nature-lovers.

2 Resorts
If you plan to stick to the south coast, choose your resort carefully. Maspalomas and Meloneras are tranquil, upmarket areas with little to offer in the way of nightlife. Neighbouring Playa del Inglés and Puerto Rico, further west, are more suited to young travellers seeking wild parties, though the latter is also popular with families. Puerto de Mogán is charming and quiet, and doesn't offer the usual attractions of large tourist resorts.

3 Reservations
Advance booking is essential in high season, and recommended year-round for rural and resort hotels; the former often have just a few rooms, while with the latter you're more likely to be able to strike a deal if you book ahead. Some budget places don't accept bookings; in that case it's wise to call at least a day in advance to check that there are rooms available.

4 High and Low Seasons
Although the island is a year-round destination, prices still rise in high season *(see p107)*. Some hotels (mainly rural and budget hotels) have fixed prices, but elsewhere rates can increase by anything from 20 to 50 per cent according to the time of year.

5 Budget Accommodation
Large resort hotels make up the bulk of the accommodation on offer on the island, though there are a few options for those who prefer not to splash out. Camping and hostels *(albergues)* offer rock-bottom prices, but are usually located far from large towns and resorts. If you want to stay in an urban area, opt for a *pensión* or *hostal*, *cheap* guesthouses with basic facilities.

6 Breakfast
In general, breakfast is included in all but the cheapest of hotels and is usually a grand buffet of cheese, cold meats, fresh fruit, cereals, yoghurt and pastries. In more upmarket places, there's also a hot breakfast, with bacon, sausages, pancakes and all manner of eggs. In rural hotels, the spread will be much smaller, but is likely to be cooked to order, and may include some local specialities.

7 Saving Water
Water is scarce on Gran Canaria, so try to conserve it wherever possible. Re-use your towels, don't leave taps running while brushing your teeth, and take a shower instead of a bath.

8 Camping
Much of Gran Canaria is protected by environmental laws. You can't just pitch your tent wherever you want to, and you must apply for a permit to use the designated camping areas *(see p107)*. Permits are free and easy to get, except on bank holiday weekends, when locals flock to the countryside. Call 928 21 94 65, and have the passport details of all campers to hand.

9 Self-catering
There are far more apartments than hotel rooms available on the island, but many of them are taken by the mighty tour operators, so in some resorts you might find it tricky to get an apartment, even in low season. Self-catering accommodation away from the resorts is quite scarce, but usually offers an excellent deal.

10 Single Rooms
It works out far more expensive to travel alone than with a partner. Most hotels charge about 70 per cent of the double tariff for single occupancy.

If you haven't booked in advance, turn up late in the evening for the best chance of bagging a bargain.

Left *Raciones* menu Right Coffee and *churros*

Top 10 Eating and Drinking Tips

1 Tapas and Raciones

Tapas are mini portions of varied cuisine, designed to accompany a beer or other drink. *Raciones* are larger portions of the same, providing enough food to make a meal for one. A *media ración* is a half-portion, and the norm is to order a few of these to share among friends; usually one less plate than the number of people is the right amount.

2 Menu del Día

A cheap yet often delicious way to fill up at lunchtime *(see p107)*.

3 Tipping

Waiters don't live on their tips in Gran Canaria, but a gratuity of 5 to 10 per cent is certainly welcome and often expected. In some restaurants the service is included, so check before tipping.

4 Vegetarians

Vegetarians will suffer on Gran Canaria, and vegans even more so. Salads appear on every menu, but they often include tuna, so you have to be specific if you want no trace of meat or fish. You'll soon tire of potatoes and omelettes, so head to an Italian restaurant for a more stimulating range of vegetarian dishes. Fish eaters will have no problems – the island is among the best places in Spain to eat *pescado*.

5 Opening Hours

Most Canarian restaurants close for a couple of hours in the afternoon; typical opening times are 1–4.30pm, then 7pm–midnight. The majority close for at least one full day each week – often Sunday, Monday or Tuesday. In top tourist spots, however, many of the restaurants stay open throughout *siesta* time, and tend not to have a closing day.

6 Large Measures

Local spirit measures are rather more generous than you might be used to at home, so it's advisable to go easy on the alcohol. The preferred local tipple is rum – more specifically, Arehucas rum, though all international brands are widely available. Ask for a *cubata* (Cuba Libre) if you really want to fit in with the natives.

7 Eat with the Locals

If you find yourself eating in an empty restaurant and are wondering why, check your watch – the Spanish eat considerably later than other European nationalities. Lunch never starts before 2pm while, at weekends, dinner can get going as late as 11pm – though 9pm is a more usual hour. Outside of the tourist resorts, you might well find that restaurants don't even open until these times.

8 Breakfast

The Canarian *desayuno* is a low-key affair, usually consisting of a pastry washed down with a cup of very strong coffee. On Sundays you'll see people clutching greasy paper bags filled with *churros*. These are large chunks of deep fried batter that you should dip in a cup of thick hot chocolate or *café con leche*.

9 Local Cuisine

Canarian cuisine is simple, but there are certain dishes that you must try while you're on the island. In winter, there's nothing better than a hearty *ropa vieja* or *potaje de berros*, especially if you're in the mountains; and leaving Gran Canaria without tasting *papas arrugadas con mojo* would be like visiting Italy and not eating pasta *(see p61)*.

10 Fish or Meat?

Your location on the island should dictate your choice of meal. On the coast, the best options are seafood and fish. Up in the mountains, chefs are more used to preparing fine cuts of meat, so you'd do well to order steak, pork or lamb. Vegetarians will probably find more salads on the coast, but vegetable stews are sometimes available in the mountains; double-check that these dishes are meat-free.

Left **Supermarket** Right **Handicrafts and embroidery on a market stall**

TOP 10 Shopping Tips

1 Siesta Time

Although larger chain stores stay open throughout the day, the majority of businesses observe the traditional Spanish timetable, closing for two or three hours in the middle of the day. Avoid shopping between 1 and 4pm, if you don't want your spree to be a washout.

2 Passports

Spanish shop assistants are thankfully rigorous about credit card use. You will not be allowed to pay with your card unless you have your passport or another form of photo ID with you.

3 Haggling

Haggling is not common practice in Gran Canaria, even in markets, and traders may well get offended if you suggest a lower price for their goods. The only people you may be able to barter with are street traders.

4 Duty-free

The amount of duty-free goods you can take home is far from generous, since in this respect the Canary Islands are not treated as part of the EU *(see p102)*. It is not advisable to leave your shopping until you get to the airport. You will make considerable savings if you buy your perfume, cigarettes and alcohol in supermarkets and department stores.

5 Handicrafts

The Canarians are rightly proud of their local crafts, and the best souvenirs you can buy are handmade ones. The north of the island is best known for its traditional knives and musical instruments, while the centre boasts basketry and pottery. Ingenio is famous for its handicrafts, with embroidery being the speciality. Markets are good places to hunt for quality wares, as are the government-run FEDAC shops.

6 Markets

Most reasonably sized towns stage some form of market on a weekly basis. Those in the southern resorts tend to specialize in bric-a-brac and cheap clothes. You should head for the central region if you are seeking something different. San Mateo, Santa Brígida, Valleseco, Teror and Las Palmas all have decent *mercadillos*, offering handicrafts and typical foodstuffs.

7 Queuing

In common with many other southern Europeans, Canarians have a loose notion of queuing. You have to be assertive if you do not want to get pushed around. When waiting to be served at, for example, a market, make a mental note of who was there before you, and speak up if someone tries to jump in. Elderly *señoras* are notorious for pushing in front of tourists, on the assumption that the language barrier will prevent them from protesting.

8 Opening Hours

Shops tend to open at around 9am or 9:30am and stay open until 1:30–2pm. After a long lunch, they reopen at 4:30pm or 5pm, and close at around 8pm. Larger shops and chain stores don't close for *siesta*, with typical hours being 10am-10pm. Virtually every shop closes on Sundays, with the exception of a few grocery stores.

9 Supermarkets

All but the smallest of *pueblos* have a supermarket selling basic provisions. In small towns, some shut for *siesta*, but those in the south and the capital stay open all day.

10 Sizes

Clothes are labelled according to the standard continental European sizes. Try everything on as Spanish clothes are often designed for narrower frames. A women's dress size 38 is equivalent to a British size 10 or a US size 8. Women's shoe sizes 38, 39, and 40 match UK 5, 6, and 6½, or US 7½, 8½, and 9. Men's shoe sizes 42, 43, and 44 translate as UK 8, 8½, and 9½, or US 8½, 9 and 10.

Be patient shopping in rural areas, where the pace of life is slow and time simply isn't an issue. For more on shopping **See pp56–7**

Left **Taxi** Right **City buses**

Top 10 Tips for Disabled Visitors

1 City Buses
Some city buses are adapted for wheelchair users, with a low floor, retractable ramp and extra space on board. All number 1 buses – on the main tourist route, crossing the city from Triana to Las Canteras – are wheelchair-friendly. For details of other routes, consult the bus company. *928 30 58 00 • www.guaguas.com*

2 Island Buses
The situation is improving, and most lines now run adapted buses at least once a day. *902 38 11 10 (timetable information) • www.globalsu.es*

3 Taxis
There are only about half a dozen wheelchair-adapted taxis, all based in Las Palmas, so you do need to book in advance. Other cabbies are usually friendly and willing to help disabled passengers. *928 46 56 66*

4 Restaurants and Museums
Access to restaurants has improved, and even many family-run eateries now have wheelchair ramps. Although most museums can be accessed, wheelchair users are sometimes limited in what they can see where there are no lifts to upper floors. Little or no information is provided for sight- or hearing-impaired travellers.

5 Towns and Resorts
Las Palmas's pavements aren't all wheelchair-friendly, and the locals do not help with their penchant for parking on them. Some of the other historic town centres have narrow, uneven streets and alleys that can also present problems. In the south, you will find things are much more up-to-date, though Puerto Rico is not the ideal resort as it clings to the side of a ravine.

6 Accommodation
As you might expect, all large upmarket hotels have ample facilities for disabled visitors, with some offering specially adapted rooms. Budget and rural accommodation is not so well prepared, rendering some country hotels inacessible. Where this applies to hotels listed in this guide *(see pp112–117)*, it is indicated at the end of an entry – but it's still advisable to check when booking.

7 Organizations
Confederación Coordinadora Estatal de Minusválidos Físicos de España (COCEMFE) is the main Spanish organization for disabled people; approach them for details of wheelchair-friendly hotels, beaches and attractions. Organización Nacional de Ciegos de España (ONCE) is an excellent national body for the visually-impaired that may be able to help with Braille maps and general travel advice. *COCEMFE: C/Lomo de las Brujas n: 1, local 7. 828 06 90 69. www.cocemfelaspalmas.org • ONCE: Avda Primero de Mayo 10. 928 43 14 11. www.once.es*

8 Online Information
There are some good English-language websites offering detailed advice for disabled travellers, including Holidays With Help and Tourism For All. *Holidays With Help: 0208 390 9752. www.holidayswithhelp.org.uk • Tourism For All: 0845 124 9971. www.tourismforall.org.uk*

9 Wheelchair Hire
Solmobility is based in the south of the island and hires out wheelchairs, scooters, walking sticks and frames. Their website also has information on hotels that have specially adapted rooms. *Solmobility: 928 73 53 11. www.solmobility.com*

10 Steps and Slopes
Gran Canaria's rugged topography stops it being a truly wheelchair-friendly destination. Some smaller villages are all steps and cobbles, and often where there are slopes, they are rather steep. Nearly all of the ancient Guanche sites are currently inaccessible to wheelchair users, as are some *miradors* (viewing points), beaches and other beauty spots.

Left **Suite Princess** Right **Hotel Las Tirajanas**

Top 10 Luxury Hotels

1 Hotel Santa Catalina, Las Palmas

This was the island's first hotel, welcoming tourists back in the late 19th century. The exquisite Neo-Canarian building is surrounded by the tranquil Parque Doramas, so it doesn't feel as if you're staying in a city at all. Elegant rooms, excellent sports facilities, a small spa and a classy restaurant attract the rich and famous to Gran Canaria's top hotel. *C/ León y Castillo 227 • Map J4 • 928 24 30 40 • www.hotelsanta catalina.com • €€€€€*

2 Hotel Sercotel Cristina, Las Palmas

The Sercotel Cristina boasts the best location in Las Palmas – just a few metres of promenade separate it from the finest area of Playa de Las Canteras – and its seafront restaurant serves some of the best seafood in the city. *C/ Gomera 6 • Map P2 • 928 26 80 50 • www. hotelcristinalaspalmas.com • €€€*

3 Hotel Fataga, Las Palmas

Located in the busy city centre and with excellent conference facilities, this is the perfect hotel for business travellers. It's also convenient for the shops and close to both beaches. *C/ Néstor de la Torre 21 • Map N3 • 928 29 06 14 • www.hotelfataga.com • €€*

4 Gran Hotel Lopesan Villa del Conde, Meloneras

You've probably never stayed anywhere quite like this. The reception building is in the style of an immense Neo-Classical Canarian church, based on the Templo Parroquial in Agüimes *(see p38)*. Around the huge, sand-bordered pool are houses inspired by varied styles of local architecture. There are excellent dining and sports facilities; indulge, then work it off. *C/ Mar Mediterráneo 7 • Map D6 • 928 56 32 00 • www. lopesanhotels.com • €€€€€*

5 Palm Beach, Maspalomas

The Palm beach features retro-styling by Parisian designer Alberto Pinto. The bedrooms are decorated with bold, clashing colours reminiscent of the 1970s. *Avda del Oasis s/n • Map D6 • 928 72 10 32 • www.hotel-palm-beach.com • €€€€€*

6 Hotel Cordial Mogán Playa, Puerto de Mogán

Every detail has been taken care of here, from the in-room DVD players to the option of renting an empty mini-bar and filling it with your own purchases. The *à la carte* restaurant is among the island's top eateries (*see p99*). *De los Marrero 2 • Map B5 • 928 72 41 00 • www.cordialcanarias. com • €€€*

7 Hotel Las Tirajanas, San Bartolomé de Tirajana

Waking up to see the mist rising over the craggy southern ravines is an unforgettable way to start the day, and the opulent rooms all offer the same breathtaking view. *C/ Oficial Mayor José Rubio • Map D4 • 928 56 69 69 • www.hotelrurallastirajanas. com • €€*

8 Seaside Grand Hotel Residencia, Maspalomas

Gran Canaria's most exclusive hotel is a real haven. Elegant rooms, exquisite restaurant and an inviting spa. *Avda del Oasis 32 • Map D6 • 928 72 31 00 • www.seaside-hotels.com • €€€€€*

9 Lopesan Baobab Resort, Meloneras

An enormous village resort, this hotel provides all you need on site – and then some! *Mar Adriatico 1 • Map C6 • 928 15 44 00 • www. lopesanhotels.com • €€€€*

10 Suite Princess, Puerto de Mogán

The breakfast and dinner buffets here are unrivalled, guaranteeing that you'll gain a few pounds during your stay. There's a large pool, and various racket sports are on offer. *Urbanización Taurito • Map B5 • 928 56 50 03 • www.princess-hotels.com • €€€*

***Note:** Unless otherwise stated, all hotels accept credit cards and have en-suite bathrooms and air conditioning*

Hotel Villa de Agüimes

Price Categories

For a standard, double room per night (with breakfast if included), taxes and extra charges.

€	under €50
€€	€50–€100
€€€	€100–€150
€€€€	€150–€200
€€€€€	over €200

Top 10 Budget Hotels

1 Hotel Igramar Canteras, Las Palmas

Perfectly located a stone's throw from the beach and a short walk away from two bustling shopping areas. Staff are professional, and the communal areas are cheerful places to while away an evening. *C/ Colombia 12 • Map G2 • 928 47 29 60 • www.igramar.com • €€*

2 Hotel Villa de Agüimes

Once home to the town hall, the charming 19th-century building now harbours a truly quaint hotel with just six bedrooms. *C/ El Sol 3 • Map E4 • 928 78 50 03 • www.hecansa.com • No air con • No disabled access • €€*

3 Pensión Juan Deniz, Puerto de Mogán

Positioned in a maze of steep alleys high above Puerto de Mogán. Rooms are basic but spotless. *Lomo Quiebre 20 • Map B5 • 928 56 55 39 • No credit cards • No en-suite • No air con • No disabled access • €*

4 Hotel Los Cascajos, La Aldea de San Nicolás

A warm welcome awaits guests at San Nicolas's oldest hotel. Rooms are simple, but comfy, clean and reasonably priced. *C/ Los Cascajos 9 • Map B3 • 928 89 11 65 • No air con • Limited disabled access • €*

5 Hotel Aloe Canteras – Tenesoya, Las Palmas

Located just off the promenade, the hotel lacks sea views, but you can smell the salt, and you're only seconds from the beach. It's a first-rate budget alternative, with professional staff and good facilities. *C/ Sagasta 98 • Map P1 • 928 46 49 07 • www.hotelaloe-canteras.com • €€*

6 Hostal Alcaravaneras, Las Palmas

Immaculate and well-run, this is a fine budget option within the city, situated in an agreeable residential area close to the Alcaravaneras beach and not far from the city centre. Not all rooms have private bathroom. *C/ Luis Antúnez 22 • Map H3 • 928 24 89 14 • No credit cards • No air con • No disabled access • €*

7 Dunas Mirador Maspalomas, Maspalomas

This good-value family hotel is close to the popular resort of Maspalomas *(see pp18–19)* and has enough facilities to keep everyone happy, including two pools and a full programme of sports and entertainment. Although it's a long way to the beach, shuttle buses provide easy access to and from the sand. *C/ Einstein • Map D6 • 928 14 18 02 • No air con • €€*

8 Aparthotel Regina Mar, Playa del Inglés

Situated in the busy heart of Playa del Inglés, this friendly place has basic rooms with TV and a rudimentary kitchen. The small pool offers a quiet place to relax, away from the crowds. *Avda de Estados Unidos 38 • Map D6 • 928 76 65 82 • No air con • €*

9 Hostal Albacar, Playa de Melenara

The Albacar is situated close to the expansive Playa de Melenara, in an area of the island that tourists rarely visit. Rooms are simple, but all have TV and en-suite bathrooms. There are some wonderful fish and seafood restaurants nearby. A good place to mix with the locals and experience the real Gran Canaria. *C/ Padre Cueto 4 • Map F3 • 928 13 15 20 • No air con • No disabled access • €*

10 IFA Hotel Continental, Playa del Inglés

The Continental is well positioned in the centre of the resort, just a few minutes' walk from the main beach. As well as two large swimming pools, there are four jacuzzis and a kids' pool with waterslide. Good sports facilities and nightly entertainment complete the picture. *Avda de Italia • Map D6 • 928 76 16 50 • www.ifacanarias.es • €€*

Left **Finca Las Longueras** Right **Hacienda del Buen Suceso**

Top 10 Rural Hotels

1 Finca Las Longueras, Valle de Agaete

This splendid, family-run 19th-century mansion with just 12 rooms is set in the stunning landscape of the Agaete Valley. *Map C2 • 928 89 81 45 • www.laslongueras.com • No air con • No disabled access • €€*

2 Hotel Rural Maipéz, La Calzada

This rural hotel has great views of the lush Guiniguada ravine, yet it's just 10 minutes from Las Palmas. Cosy, elegantly decorated rooms, pleasant gardens and a good restaurant serving traditional food. *Ctra La Calzada 104 • Map E2 • 928 28 72 72 • www.hotelmaipez.com • No air con • €€*

3 Hotel El Mondalón, Marzagan

This boutique hotel is as popular with hikers, given that you can walk to Caldera de Bandama from here, as it is with those who are inclined to recline by the Mondalón's swimming pool. *GC801 • Map F2 • 928 35 57 858 • €€€*

4 Hacienda del Buen Suceso, Arucas

Set amongst extensive banana plantations, this splendid mansion offers a perfect blend of peace, luxury and rural charm. Gym, jacuzzi and excellent restaurant. *Arucas to Bañaderos road km 1 • Map D2 • 928 62 29 45 • www.haciendabuensuceso.com • No air con • €€€*

5 Hotel Rural Casa de los Camellos, Agüimes

Though based in the quiet town centre of Agüimes, this is classed as a rural hotel because of its wonderful rustic interior. Formerly a granary and camel stables, it's been fully restored and has an award-winning restaurant serving local cuisine. *C/ Progreso 12 • Map E4 • 928 78 50 03 • www.hecansa.com • No air con • No disabled access • €€*

6 El Refugio, Cruz de Tejeda

The cosy rooms are most inviting in winter, when the area is cloaked in a chilling fog. In summer, guests can enjoy the sunshine around the small pool. Perfectly placed for hikers and anyone who wants to get to know the centre of the island. *Cruz de Tejeda s/n • Map D3 • 928 66 65 13 • www.hotelruralelrefugio.com • No disabled access • €€*

7 Hacienda de Anzo, Vega de Anzo

Far from the crowds, this restored mansion offers good views of the Guía skyline and the interior mountains. The dining terrace and swimming pool are bordered by beautiful gardens. A huge cave is used for meetings and celebrations. *Near Guía • Map C1 • 928 55 16 55 • www.hotelhaciendadeanzo.es • No air con • No disabled access • €€*

8 Hotel El Cortijo San Ignacio Golf, Telde

A family-run 18th-century house a stone's throw from the El Cortijo golf course. There's a huge swimming pool surrounded by palm trees, and a small chapel. *GC1, km 6.4 • Map F3 • 928 71 24 27 • www.cortijosanignacio golf.com • No air con • €€*

9 Hotel Rural Las Calas, San Mateo

This splendid traditional building in an out-of-the-way village has just six rooms, each individually decorated. Ideal if you want to explore the central mountains or just get away from it all. *C/ El Arenal 36, La Lechuza • Map D3 • 928 66 14 36 • www.hotelrurallas calas.com • No air con • €€*

10 Hotel Rural Villa del Monte, Santa Brígida

The traditional exterior gives no hint of what lies within: an explosion of contemporary decor and tropical plants. *C/ Castaño Bajo 9 • Map E3 • 928 64 43 89 • No credit cards • No air con • Limited disabled access • €€*

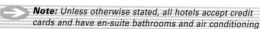

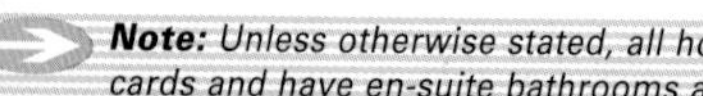

***Note:** Unless otherwise stated, all hotels accept credit cards and have en-suite bathrooms and air conditioning*

Gran Hotel Lopesan Costa Meloneras

Price Categories

For a standard, double room per night (with breakfast if included), taxes and extra charges.

€	under €50
€€	€50–€100
€€€	€100–€150
€€€€	€150–€200
€€€€€	over €200

Top 10 Spa Hotels

1 Eugenia Victoria, Playa del Inglés

The hotel may be less exclusive than some of its peers, but its spa is one of the best equipped. Enjoy tennis and squash courts, mini golf and a gym. *Avda de Gran Canaria 26 • Map D6 • 928 76 25 00 • www.bullhotels.com • €€*

2 Hotel Puerto de las Nieves, Puerto de las Nieves

The oldest hotel in town is a peaceful place to relax and enjoy the small but perfectly-equipped spa. Dozens of beauty treat-ments are available, and some specially designed programs lasting two or three days. *Avda Alcalde José de Armas • Map B2 • 928 88 62 56 • www.hotelpuertodelasnieves.es • €€€*

3 Gloria Palace Amadores, Amadores

The ocean view from the rooftop pool is amazing. There are two beaches within walking distance, a large terrace, excellent leisure facilities and a thalassotherapy circuit. *C/ La Palma 2 • Map B5 • 928 12 85 05 • www.gloriapalaceth.com • €€€*

4 Gran Hotel Lopesan Costa Meloneras, Maspalomas

The fabulous spa at this massive complex is perhaps the island's best. It's certainly the biggest, with a four-hour circuit of steam rooms, saunas, massaging showers and, for the brave, an igloo. Many rooms have sea views, as does the vast swimming pool. *C/ Mar Mediterráneo 1 • Map D6 • 928 12 81 00 • www.lopesanhr.com • €€€€*

5 Meliá Tamarindos, San Agustín

If you don't want to have to leave your hotel, this is the ideal place to stay. Rooms are bright and airy, the spa is excellent, and there are dozens of beauty treatments on offer. The adjoining casino has nightly cabaret shows and the restaurant is outstanding. *C/ Retama 3 • Map D6 • 928 77 40 90 • www.solmelia.com • €€€*

6 Palm Beach, Maspalomas

In a quiet corner of the spa, medical staff offer curative treatments alongside the usual beauty therapies. The *à la carte* restaurant is a cut above most hotel dining rooms. *Avda del Oasis • Map D6 • 928 72 10 32 • www.seaside-hotels.com • €€€€€*

7 Hotel Puerto de Mogán, Puerto de Mogán

Perched at the end of the marina, the hotel has direct access straight into the ocean via steps leading from the pool terrace. The rooms have wonderful views, either of the harbour or out to sea. Compact spa and scuba diving school. *3E, Urbanización Puerto de Mogán s/n • Map B5 • 928 56 50 66 • www.hotelpuertodemogan.com • €€*

8 Gloria Palace San Agustín

The island's first thalassotherapy centre and still one of the biggest, demanding two hours for the full circuit. Quietly situated away from the hectic resort centre, it's still convenient for beach, shopping and casino. *C/ De las Magnolias • Map D6 • 928 77 64 04 • www.gloriapalaceth.com • €€€*

9 Vital Suites, Playa del Inglés

Serenity reigns at this intimate spa with views over the golf course and sand dunes. Accommodation is in large, bright suites grouped around well-kept gardens. If you crave excitement, the busy resort centre is just a 10-minute walk away. *Avda Gran Canaria 80 • Map D6 • 928 73 02 33 • www.vitalsuites.com • €€€*

10 H10 Meloneras Palace, Meloneras

The friendly staff at this large, spacious hotel offer guests a judicious selection of reasonably-priced wellness treatments. There's easy access to the Meloneras beach and shopping centre. *C/ Mar Caspio 5 • Map D6 • 928 12 82 82 • www.h10.es • €€€€*

Left **Guantánamo, Tauro** Right **Albergue Centro Internacional de Windsurfing**

Top 10 Campsites and Hostels

1 Camping Villamar, Tasartico

This friendly, well-run site in the remotest region of the island has cabins and caravans as well as space to pitch tents. Facilities include a restaurant and a bar. It's close to the start of the Güigüí hike *(see pp82–3)*, and a short walk from a quiet, pebbly beach. *Tasartico to Playa del Asno road • Map A4 • 696 92 41 63 • €*

2 Camping Guantánamo, Tauro

There are three campsites in this group, one on the coast and two further up the ravine, all with good facilities and well located for the southern resorts without being in the midst of it all. The pretty location has been slightly marred by year-round campers building makeshift houses. *Playa de Tauro • Map B5 • 928 56 20 98 • €*

3 Hostal Alcaravaneras, Las Palmas

Basic but comfy is the best way to describe this hostel. One major advantage is its location – close to the two main beaches of the city. Being in the city centre also means that shopping and other facilities are close at hand. Free Internet access and Wi-Fi available. *C/ Luis Antúnes 22 • Map H3 • 928 24 89 14 • www.canaryhostel.com • €*

4 Cabildo Campsites

These sites are basic – most are just clearings where you can pitch your tent – but they are free, and scattered about in some of the island's top locations. You must phone in advance for permission. *928 21 94 21*

5 Camping Playa de Vargas

Located on a sports beach, this is the perfect base for kitesurfers and windsurfers. Close to the airport, Camping Playa de Vargas can accommodate up to 500 campers. *Playa de Vargas • Map F4 • 928 18 80 37 • €*

6 Albergue La Hoyilla, La Aldea de San Nicolás

The enthusiastic management keep rooms and dormitories spotless. Breakfast is included in the price. Kitchen facilities available. *C/ Barran- quillo las Planchas s/n • Map B3 • 928 89 12 52 • €*

7 Albergue Centro Internacional de Windsurfing, Pozo Izquierdo

Swim in the large pool, take diving lessons, enjoy various adrenaline sports and, of course, learn to windsurf. The dormitory-style accommodation is basic but clean. There is also a recreation area with TV and board games. *Playa Pozo Izquierdo • Map E5 • 928 12 14 00 • www.pozo-ciw.com • €*

8 Refugio Cañada del Escobón, Llanos de la Pez

This basic shelter in the picturesque centre of the island is run by the Gran Canarian Mountaineering Association. It's ideal for hikers and climbers, but offers little more than minimal kitchen facilities, water and electricity. Take your own bedding. The key has to be collected from and returned to the office in Las Palmas. *Map D3 • Federación Gran Canaria de Montañismo: C/Mari Sánchez 18. 928 46 00 45 www.fgcm.org • €*

9 Camping Temisas

This well-equipped site is close enough to the south for a day trip to the beach, but sufficiently off the beaten track to make you feel as if you're on another island. For those who have no tent, there are cabins. *Lomo de la Cruz 27, off GC551 • Map E4 • 928 79 81 49 • €*

10 Refugio de San Bernardo

This simple shelter at the island's highest point offers spectacular views, but it can get extremely cold, so come prepared. *Nr Pico de las Nieves • Map D3 • Booking details and facilities as 8 above*

Most of the campsites and hostels listed above have limited or no disabled access and do not take credit cards.

Apartamentos Brisamar

Price Categories

For a standard, double room per night (with breakfast if included), taxes and extra charges.	
€	under €50
€€	€50–€100
€€€	€100–€150
€€€€	€150–€200
€€€€€	over €200

TOP 10 Self-catering

1 Apartamentos Brisamar, Las Palmas

You can't beat the location of these simple, studio-style apartments on the Las Canteras promenade. All balconies face the sea. *Paseo de Las Canteras 49 • Map N2 • 928 26 94 00 • www.brisamarcanteras.com • No air con • €€*

2 La Venecia de Canarias, Puerto de Mogán

There are few more serene and enchanting places to stay than this Canarian "Venice". The apartments are not lavish, but they have all the basics, plus a delightful location in Mogán's bougainvillea-clad harbour. *Urb. Puerto de Mogán 328 • Map B5 • 928 56 56 00 • www.laveneciadecanarias.net • No air con • €€*

3 Bungalows Tajaraste, Playa del Inglés

The objective here is tranquillity. Perfectly located near the dunes but away from noisy night-life, the bungalows have well-equipped kitchens but no TV. The two pools are set in marvellous gardens. *C/ Finlandia 4 • Map D6 • 928 76 00 64 • www.tajarastebungalows.com • No air con • €€*

4 Casas Rurales

Many of these magnificent, fully equipped self-catering cottages are located in spectacular locations. Numerous agencies arrange stays here; the two listed below offer the greatest choice. *Gran Canaria Rural: 928 46 44 64. www.grancanariarural.com. €€ • Gran Tural: 928 39 01 69. www.ecoturismocanarias.com. €€*

5 Cave houses, Artenara

These man-made caves offer an original spin on the rural holiday cottage. The heated grottoes offer all home comforts, so it's not quite the Guanche experience, but it's certainly something to tell your friends about. *Map C3 • Artenatur: 686 79 58 49. www.artenatur.com.*

6 Villas Blancas, Maspalomas

Numerous establishments in the area offer accommodation exclusively to gay men; this is one of the most popular. Each bungalow has its own private sun terrace, and there's a communal gym, pool, bar and restaurant. *Avda Touroperador Tjaereborg • Map D6 • www.villas blancas.com • €€*

7 Finca Las Tortolas, Cercados de Araña

If you want to go off the beaten track, try these simple, cosy apartments next to the Presa de Chira *(see p96)*. The island's largest reservoir is an excellent place to fish for carp, while the surrounding area is perfect for hiking. *Map C4 • 928 12 90 60 • chirafish@hotmail.com • No credit cards • No air con • €*

8 Atlantia Resorts

This local company has quiet, low-lying complexes of apartments and bungalows scattered around the San Agustín to Maspalomas area. They even have apartments to let out in Las Palmas. *Map D6 • C/ Las Adelfas 5 (San Agustin): 928 77 71 23. www.grupoatlantia.com. €€*

9 Apartamentos Gayfa, Tejeda

These spacious, well-kept apartments have a good-sized kitchen, TV, four beds and a large balcony. Take plenty of clothing if you visit in winter – it gets chilly up here, and the heating is somewhat ineffective. *General highway, Tejeda • Map C3 • 928 66 62 30 • No credit cards • No air con • No disabled access • €*

10 Apartamentos Faro Sardina

Next to Sardina's light-house and close to the port and beach, these spotless, spacious modern apartments have large terraces with magnificent sea views. Advance book-ings only. *Avda Santiago Quevedo Megías • Map C1 • 626 29 71 01 • No credit cards • No air con • €*

General Index

Acknowledgements

'he Author
.ucy Corne has written in depth on he Canaries, and this is her second uide to the islands. She also works s a freelance writer, contributing ravel articles to a variety of ublications. When not writing, she nakes a living teaching English.

huge gracias to Hector Sanchez,)avid Bramwell and the cheery staff f the island's tourist information ffices, particularly those in Teror and ;áldar. Thanks also to multitudes of otel staff, and to the residents of hose towns too small to have their wn information point.

pecial thanks for her invaluable ssistance to Juana Rosa Alemán at 'atronato de Turismo de Gran Canaria.

'roduced by DP Services, a division f DUNCAN PETERSEN PUBLISHING TD, 31 Ceylon Road, London W14 0PY
ditorial Director Chris Barstow
esigner Ian Midson
opy Editors Jane Egginton, Jane)liver-Jedrzejak
icture Researcher Lily Sellar
act-checkers Aday Tejedor Betancor, oe Cawley, Matthew Hirtes
ndexer Hilary Bird
roofreader Yoko Kawaguchi
lain Photographer Antony Souter
dditional Photography Linda Vhitwam, Kim Sayer, Pawel Wojcik, eville Walker
lustrator Chapel Design & Marketing
laps John Plumer (JP Map raphics Ltd)

artography Credits Gran Canaria ase map derived from Gran Canaria ourist Board, www.grancanaria. om. Las Palmas base map derived om Distrimapas, Spain.

OR DORLING KINDERSLEY
ublishing Manager Kate Poole
enior Art Editor Tessa Bindloss
lanaging Editor Fay Franklin
enior Cartographic Editor Casper lorris
TP Jason Little
roduction Stuart Masheter

Revisions Team Sreemoyee Basu, Marta Bescos, Stuti Tiwari Bhatia, Nadia Bonomally, Joe Cawley, Anna Freiberger, Sumita Khatwani, Sonal Modha, Helen Partington, Beverly Smart, Ajay Verma

Picture Credits
Key: a-above; b-below/bottom; c-centre; f-far; l-left; r-right; t-top.

The publishers would like to thank the following individuals, companies and picture libraries for permission to reproduce their photographs:

AISA ARCHIVO ICONOGRÁFICO: 34c. ALAMY IMAGES: Alan Dawson Photography 30cb; Cris Haigh 30bc. AQUA OCEAN CLUB: 98tr. ARCHIVO DE FOTOGRAFÍA HISTÓRICA DE LA FEDAC: 34t, 35cl, 35br.

LAS BRUJAS: 70tr.

CASA DE GALICIA RESTAURANTE: 61cl. CASA MUSEO ANTONIO PADRÓN: 36b. CASA MUSEO DE COLÓN: 6c, 8tl, 8cb, 8b, 9t, 9cr, 9bl, 58tr.

EMPICS: 47r

HOTEL RURAL LAS TIRAJANAS: 85tl.

JARDÍN BOTÁNICO CANARIO: 16tc, 16tr, 17bl, 17br.

ORONOZ: 34b.

PATRONATO DE TURISMO DE GRAN CANARIA: 2tl, 4–5c, 6clb, 7tl, 10tl, 18–19c, 19cr, 20–21c, 42tr, 44cl, 45t, 47cl, 51br, 54tl, 54tr, 54c, 54br, 55cl, 55tr, 55br, 64cl, 77cl, 80c, 97r, 107tl.

TEATRO CUYS: 70tl.

TIENDA ARTESANIA CANARIA LAS PALMITAS: 56bl.

WWW.SPAIN-GRANCANARIA.COM (THE GRAN CANARIA HOLIDAY DESTINATION GUIDE): 102tr.

Phrase Book

In an Emergency

Help!	**¡Socorro!**	soh-koh-roh
Stop!	**¡Pare!**	pah-reh
Call a doctor.	**¡Llame a un médico!**	yah-meh ah oon meh-de-koh
Call an ambulance.	**¡Llame a una ambulancia!**	yah-meh ah ahm-boo-lahn-see-ah
Call the police.	**¡Llame a la policía!**	yah-meh ah lah poh-lee-see-ah
Call the fire brigade.	**¡Llame a los bomberos!**	yah-meh ah lohs bohm-beh-rohs

Communication Essentials

Yes/No	**Sí/No**	see/noh
Please	**Por favor**	pohr fah-vorh
Thank you	**Gracias**	grah-see-ahs
Excuse me	**Perdone**	pehr-doh-neh
Hello	**Hola**	oh-lah
Goodbye	**Adiós**	ah-dee-ohs
Good night	**Buenas noches**	bweh-nahs noh-chehs
What?	**¿Qué?**	keh?
When?	**¿Cuando?**	kwan-doh?
Why?	**¿Por qué?**	pohr-keh?
Where?	**¿Dónde?**	dohn-deh?

Useful Phrases

How are you?	**Cómo está usted?**	koh-moh ehs-tah oos-tehd
Very well, . thank you.	**Muy bien, gracias.**	mwee bee-ehn grah-see-ahs
Pleased to meet you.	**Encantado/a de cononcerle.**	ehn-kahn-tah-doh deh koh-noh-sehr-leh
That's fine.	**Está bien.**	ehs-tah bee-ehn
Where is/are ...?	**¿Dónde está/están?**	dohn-deh ehs-tah/ehs-tahn
Which way to ...?	**¿Por dónde se va a ...?**	pohr dohn-deh seh bah ah
Do you speak English?	**¿Habla inglés?**	ah-blah een-glehs
I don't understand.	**No comprendo.**	noh kom-prehn-doh
I'm sorry.	**Lo siento.**	loh see-ehn-toh

Shopping

How much does this cost?	**¿Cuánto cuesta esto?**	kwahn-toh kwehs-tah ehs-toh
I would like ...	**Me gustaría ...**	meh goos-ta-ree-ah
Do you have ...?	**¿Tienen ...?**	tee-yeh-nehn
Do you take credit cards?	**¿Aceptan tarjetas de crédito?**	ah-sehp-tan tahr-heh-tas-deh kreh-deee-toh
What time do you open/close?	**A qué hora abren/cierran?**	ah keh oh-rah ah-brehn/see-ehr-rahn
this one/that one	**éste/ése**	ehs-teh/eh-seh
expensive	**caro**	kahr-oh
cheap	**barato**	bah-rah-toh
size (clothes)	**talla**	tah-yah
size (shoes)	**número**	noo-mehr-roh
white	**blanco**	blahn-koh
black	**negro**	neh-groh
red	**rojo**	roh-hoh
yellow	**amarillo**	ah-mah-ree-yoh
green	**verde**	behr-deh
blue	**azul**	ah-zool
bakery	**la panadería**	lah pah-nah-deh-ree-ah
bank	**el banco**	ehl bahn-koh
bookshop	**la librería**	lah lee-breh-ree-ah
cake shop	**la pastelería**	lah pahs-teh-leh-ree-ah
chemist	**la farmacia**	lah fahr-mah-see-ah
grocer's	**la tienda de de comestibles**	lah tee-yehn-dah deh koh-mehs-tee-blehs
hairdresser	**la peluquería**	lah peh-loo-keh-ree-ah
market	**el mercado**	ehl mehr-kah-doh
newsagent	**el kiosko de prensa**	ehn kee-ohs-koh deh prehn-sah
supermarket	**el supermercado**	ehl soo-pehr-mehr-kah-doh
travel agency	**la agencia de viaje**	lah ah-hehn-see-ah deh bee-ah-heh

Sightseeing

art gallery	**la galería de arte**	lah gah-leh-ree-ah duh ah-teh
bus station	**la estación de guaguas**	lah ehs-tah-ee-ohn deh wah-wah
cathedral	**la catedral**	lah kah-teh-drahl
church	**la iglesia/la basílica**	lah ee-gleh-see-ah/lah bah-seel i-kah
closed for holidays	**cerrado por vacaciones**	sehr-rah-doh porhr bah-kah-cee-oh-nehs
garden	**el jardín**	ehl hahr-deen
museum	**el museo**	ehl moo-seh-oh
tourist information	**la oficina de turismo**	lah oh-fee-see-nah deh too-rees-moh

Eating Out

Have you got a table for ...?	**¿Tienen mesa para ... ?**	Tee-eh-nehn meh-sah pah-rah
I'd like to reserve a table.	**Quiero reservar una mesa.**	kee-eh-roh reh-sehr-bahr oo-nah meh-sah
breakfast	**el desayuno**	ehl deh-sah-yoo-noh
lunch	**la comida/el almuerzo**	lah koh-mee-dah/ehl ahl-mwehr-soh
dinner	**la cena**	lah seh-nah
The bill, please.	**La cuenta, por favor.**	lah kwehn-tah pohr fah-vohr
waiter/waitress	**camerero/camerera**	kah-mah-reh-roh kah-mah-reh-rah
fixed price menu	**menú del día**	meh-noo dehl dee-ah
dish of the day	**el plato del día**	ehl plah-toh dehl dee-ah
starters	**los entremeses**	lohs ehn-treh-meh-sehs
main course	**el primer plato**	ehl pree-mehr plah-toh
glass	**un vaso**	oon bah-soh

ottle	**una botella**	oon-nah boh-teh-yah
ne list	**la carta de vinos**	lah kahr-tah deh bee-nohs
ife	**un cuchillo**	oon koo-chee-yoh
rk	**un tenedor**	oon te-neh-dohr
oon	**una cuchara**	oon-ah koo-chah-rah
ffee	**el café**	ehl kah-feh
re	**poco hecho**	poh-koh eh-choh
edium	**medio hecho**	meh-dee-oh eh-choh
ell done	**muy hecho**	mwee eh-choh

taying in a Hotel

o you have y vacant oms?	**¿Tienen una habitación libre?**	tee-eh-nehn oo-nah ah-bee-tah see-ohn lee-breh
uble room	**Habitación doble**	ah-bee-tah-see-ohn dob-bleh
th double bed	**con cama de matrimonio**	kohn kah-mah deh mah-tree-moh-nee-oh
in room	**Habitación con dos camas**	ah-bee-tah-see-ohn kohn dohs kah-mahs
ngle room	**Habitación individual**	ah-bee-tah-see-ohn een-dee-vee-doo-ahl
om with a th/shower	**Habitación con baño/ducha**	ah-bee-tah-see-ohn kohn bah-nyoh/doo-chah
ave a servation.	**Tengo una habitación reservada.**	tehn-goh oo-na ah-bee-tah-see-ohn reh-sehr-bah-dah

enu Decoder

horno	ahl ohr-noh	baked
ado	ah-sah-do	roast
aceite	ah-see-eh-teh	oil
eitunas	ah-seh-toon-ahs	olives
agua mineral	ah-gwal mee-neh-rah	mineral water
n gas/con gas	seen gas/kohn gas	still/sparkling
ajo	ah-hoh	garlic
arroz	ahr-rohs	rice
azúcar	ah-soo-kahr	sugar
carne	kahr-ne	meat
cebolla	ceh-boh-yah	onion
cerveza	sehr-beh-sah	beer
cerdo	sehr-doh	pork
chocolate	choh-koh-lah-te	chocolate
chorizo	choh-ree-soh	red sausage
cordero	kohr-deh-roh	lamb
fiambre	fee-ahm-breh	cold meat
to	free-toh	fried
fruta	froo-tah	fruit
s frutos secos	frooh-tohs seh-kohs	nuts
s gambas	gahm-bas	prawns
helado	eh-lah-doh	ice-cream
huevo	oo-eh-voh	egg
jamón	hah-mohn	cured ham
rano	sehr-rah-noh	
jerez	heh-rehz	sherry
langosta	lahn-gohs-tah	lobster
la leche	leh-cheh	milk
el limón	lee-mohn	lemon
la limonada	lee-moh-nah-dah	lemonade
la mantequilla	mahn-teh-kee-yah	butter
la manzana	mahn-tsah-nah	apple
los mariscos	mah-rees-kohs	shellfish
la menestra	meh-nehs-trah	vegetable stew
la naranja	nah-rahn-hah	orange
el pan	pahn	bread
el pastel	pahs-tehl	cake
las patatas	pah-tah-tas	potatoes
el pescado	pehs-kah-doh	fish
la pimienta	pee-mee-yehn-tah	pepper
el plátano	plah-tah-noh	banana
el pollo	poh-yoh	chicken
el postre	pohs-treh	dessert
el queso	keh-soh	cheese
la sal	sahl	salt
las salchichas	sahl-chee-chahs	sausages
la salsa	sahl-sa	sauce
seco	seh-koh	dry
el solomillo	soh-loh-mee yoh	sirloin
la sopa	soh-pah	soup
la tarta	tahr-ta	tart
el té	teh	tea
la ternera	tehr-neh-rah	beef
las tostadas	tohs-tah-dahs	toast
el vinagre	bee-nah-gre	vinegar
el vino blanco	bee-noh blahn-koh	white wine
el vino rosado	bee-noh roh-sah-doh	rosé wine
el vino tinto	bee-noh teen-toh	red wine

Numbers

0	**cero**	seh-roh
1	**un**	oon-noh
2	**dos**	dohs
3	**tres**	trehs
4	**cuatro**	kwa troh
5	**cinco**	seen-koh
6	**seis**	says
7	**siete**	see-eh-teh
8	**ocho**	oh-choh
9	**nueve**	nweh-veh
10	**diez**	dee-ehs
11	**once**	ohn-seh
12	**doce**	doh-seh
13	**trece**	treh-seh
14	**catorce**	kah-tohr-seh
15	**quince**	keen-seh
16	**dieciseis**	dee-eh-see-seh-ess
17	**diecisiete**	dee-eh-see-see-eh-teh
18	**dieciocho**	dee-eh-see-oh-choh
19	**diecinueve**	dee-eh-see-newh-veh
20	**veinte**	beh-een-teh
30	**treinta**	treh-een-tah
40	**cuarenta**	kwah-rehn-tah
50	**cincuenta**	seen-kwehn-tah
60	**sesenta**	seh-sehn-tah
70	**setenta**	seh-tehn-tah
80	**ochenta**	oh-chehn-tah
90	**noventa**	noh-vehn-tah
100	**cien**	seh-ehn
1000	**mil**	meel
1001	**mil uno**	meel oo-noh

Gran Canaria: Selected Index of Places